Sell Futures, Not Features

Michael Killen

DEDICATION

To Mum, who taught me that there is nothing so awful that it can't be fixed if you share it with family. X

TABLE OF CONTENTS

ACKNOWLEDGMENTS

I'd like to thank every member of the Sell Your Service community for sticking with me during 2021. It's been a rough few years for everyone, and I've seen true resilience, grit and selflessness from all of you. Your kind words though my illness and support while I took lots of time off hasn't gone unnoticed.

And to my team at Sell Your Service, thank you for allowing me to take the time off to recover while keeping the business going. I think it says a lot about my management style and how great you all are at your jobs, that we had our best year ever while I was nowhere near the business. You all took on extra work, made great decisions and I will be forever grateful.

Chapter 1 – I'm a fraud and a liar

There were six of us including myself sat round a table in an exclusive London members club, with a prominent millionaire business owner at the head of the table. We had won a private full day's workshop with him. He is an author, business leader, influencer and a great speaker. He is also focused, disciplined but calm and approachable. Many of you would have read his books, even bought his classes and seminars. I was still pinching myself that I had managed to win some time with him. I assumed that there had been a mistake. That I was here by accident. No way did I deserve to spend time with this group of people.

I'm a fraud and a liar

The workshop was a pretty intense look at our businesses, finances, sales and messaging. It was as exhilarating as it was revealing. There was nowhere to hide, hence my fears about being "discovered". To even get into the wider membership, I had to lie about how much my business was making. I was already out of my depth and then when I won the private workshop, it was a feeling of excitement mixed with blinding fear.

What I was feeling, I was later told, is called "imposter

1

syndrome". The phenomenon that people will uncover you as a fraud and expose you to the wider world. What exacerbated the feeling of being a fraud and imposter, was that the competition to win the private workshop wasn't even based on pure luck. If I had won because of pure dumb luck, like my name being picked from a hat, I could feel a little better. I wasn't in control of that.

Instead, I along with everyone else in that room, won because I did a small work assignment based off the larger program I was a part of. We were all members of a larger 10-month program. There were a few hundred participants in this particular cohort and of that entire group, me and five other members won a private group coaching session. The rules to enter were pretty simple. Set up five partnership calls or meetings to promote your product or service. That was all. They didn't even need to pan out. You just needed to get the ball rolling. I just had to reach out to five different people and partner with them on SOMETHING to help my business.

And therein lies my problem. Setting up those partnerships took less than one hour. I made a list of people I wanted to partner with, emailed/texted/messaged them all and waited. We had one month to complete the assignment and submit our results. I sent about 20 different people messages and two got back to me within the hour. Another two by the end of the day. The last one was a few days later. I took screenshots of the conversations, emailed it to the program leaders and a few days later was told I had won the workshop. One of those partnerships was Dave Foy who wrote the forward to my last book, Five Figure Funnels. Two of them landed me speaking events where I would give a talk. The other two were promotions for my products via webinars to their audience.

I was overjoyed that I had won. But I was hit by a stark realisation that there had to have been some mistake. I didn't have to work that hard. It wasn't a grind. It was literally a few minutes work. So I started to panic. I worried that they'd mistaken my conversations as huge multi-million-pound deals. Or maybe they got my name mixed up with someone else. Or what if they thought each screenshot was another new partnership? What if they thought the people I reached out to were bigger deals than they really were? I was swimming in hypotheticals and when the day arrived and it became my turn to talk, I presumed that they'd tell me "Mike, you need to leave. You don't deserve to be here." Instead, I was asked "so Mike, how can we help your business?"

As the day went on we all worked on our own and each other's businesses. It was so powerful, so constructive. Later at lunch I built up the courage to ask how I managed to win. I didn't have to work hard. It was easy. Clearly there had been a mistake. "Mike, you and the others here were the only ones that entered."

Sell Futures, Not Features

I couldn't believe it. Out of HUNDREDS of members, almost all of whom were way more qualified than I to make use of private time with one of our idols, there were six applicants. 6/200. That's a 3% submission rate. I literally stood there, mouth agape at the answer. He continued "it happens every year. I don't take it personally anymore. If anything, it's proof that people idolise me and put me on a pedestal. They don't believe they're worthy or capable of spending time with me, or even winning, so they don't try. That's the strange thing about being at the top. They say it's lonely, but that's because no one else even tries."

Lonely at the top

He went on to explain the phenomenon of competition bias. If we covet something, we assume that everyone desires it and therefore, we believe we don't have a chance to get it. Even just thinking about the odds of winning, we believe that there is so much competition out there for the top spot or "for the win" that we don't even give it a go. Coupled with our own insecurities where we tell ourselves that we don't even deserve a place at the top, we write off our chances of success before we even start. Finally, he explained that most people assume that other people don't want to partner with them, so they never try. Despite never seeing any evidence or rejection, most people assume that partnering with bigger names/brands is something other people do.

4

Sell Futures, Not Features

He also asked me to look back at things which people are impressed with, when I show them or tell them. Interviewing Ryan Deiss, getting on a call with Mark Cuban, getting a book published. My answer to all of them was "I basically sent an email." No tricks, no hacks, no hidden networks. I don't have a wealthy family or a well-connected friend. I just did the first thing that I thought would work.

Tim Ferriss in his book 4 Hour Work Week writes about talking to a load of Princeton students on getting interviews or emails with super-wealthy successful people. He gave a similar competition to that class and explained he would buy a round-the-world ticket to anyone who got an "elite" to answer three questions. Out of 60 students who Tim spoke to, 20 met him to get the rules of the challenge. How many people won a free ticket? Zero. No one even tried. Excuses were either belief that there would be too much competition or that the task was impossible. The key takeaway for me there, is that higher peaks have fewer climbers. If I wanted to make life easier, I'd need to set my expectations unreasonably high.

It was during that day's coaching that the phrase Sell Futures, Not Features was canonized. I had been playing around with it and testing it in a few places. But when I spoke the words, the phrase just clicked. From there it's grown into a book, course, software, speaking events and workshops. It's created an income and lifestyle for me that allowed me to take

Sell Futures, Not Features

9 months off during 2021 to recover from testicular cancer.

People bring products and services to me which they know work, and can get results. But they struggle to convince other people. They struggle to convince customers that this product is perfect for them. The business owner plays down the impact to some extent and doesn't like to "hype" what they're doing. They want more sales, but they don't want to seem overly confident, pushy or tacky. After spending a few minutes with me using the Sell Futures, Not Features framework, they can see the depth of their product. They become excited and enthusiastic about it again. Maybe for the first time. They stop building their sales approach by what the product is, and start selling by what it does for the lives of their customers.

Businesses have a weird competition bias for their own products and services. We all have imposter syndrome about our own businesses and what we sell. I was a bag of nerves when I pitched the idea of Sell Futures Not Features, because "who am I to tell people how to sell their own products?" What I learned is that 90% of people are never ever ever going to care or even hear about you. 5% will love you. 5% will hate you. No matter what you create or produce, even if it helps people and saves lives, you're always going to have Zeds who are negative towards you. But you will also have super-fans, influencers, creators and evangelists who love what you do and always will. Sell Futures Not Features is my method for helping YOU overcome your fears of rejection, find people who love your product and uncover hidden desirable benefits, to your products and services, that are SO compelling, you can't help but sell them.

I later learned that everyone in the group felt the exact same way I did. Everyone thought they were a fraud for being there. Everyone had imposter syndrome. We all suffer from a small doubt that our products and services aren't that important. But from years of research, teaching and creating, I can tell you that what you sell DOES help people. You're changing lives. You're making people's lives easier and better. And that is what you should be promoting and talking about. It's 100x more interesting to talk about your customer's future and life, rather than your own product. And yet that's also the best sales method around. Three years later I still meet with that same group, every Friday morning on Zoom to talk about our businesses and work with each other. I see first-hand how a small group of people are changing lives across the world (literally) and in their own homes.

This book is to help you create better futures for your customers and network. I don't have doubts about your ability to deliver or do the work. Most people are amazing "workers" and deliver amazing products, but they struggle to make the sale. That's what I'm here to help you do – sell futures, not features.

Throughout this book, you'll find exercises that will help you build out your products, messaging, sales process and sales copy. If you'd like to download our free 9 part workbook, head over to

sellfuturesnotfeatures.com/workbook and get the entire workbook sent straight to your email for free.

Have courage, commit and take action.

Mike Killen

Chapter 2 - The Sales Process

Sell Futures, Not Features

Before we dive in, I want to share the Sell Futures, Not Features model. How we turn even the most boring products and services into hyper desirable and compelling offers that are so exciting, you can't help but sell more of them. Let's break this down.

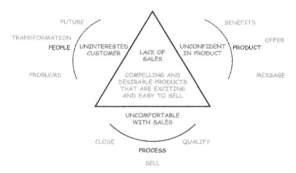

Figure

1: Sell Futures, Not Features framework

The big problem that entrepreneurs, business owners and product creators face, especially if you're reading this book, is a lack of sales. What we want to work towards is not just more sales. It's an approach to how we're going to get more sales. Everyone wants more sales, but how do we get there? And what we're specifically looking for is to create exciting and enthusiastic sales.

What we're looking to do is create compelling and desirable products that are exciting (for you to sell) and easy to sell. Which sounds like a bit of a tall order, but I promise you that when you really care about what it is that you do, and you understand how it helps people, it's actually much easier to make sales.

Figure 2: The core problem and result

And I believe that summed up, there are three basic roadblocks to why people feel this way.

We have uninterested customers. We are unconfident in the product. And we are uncomfortable with sales. Uninterested customers means when you talk to people, even if you manage to find them, they don't seem particularly interested in what it is that you're selling.

You might think "I know that this works" but it can

10

become a bit of a negative feedback cycle. Where, because it appears, you have uninterested customers, you become unconfident in the product. Because you're unconfident in the product, you become uncomfortable with sales. And because you're uncomfortable with sales, your customers seem uninterested, and it can be a bit of a doom spiral.

Figure 3: Why you're lacking sales

The way that I want to fix this for you, is by first of all, focusing not on what you're selling, but we're going to focus on the People who you're selling to. This is by focusing on the customer – the People. When it comes to feeling unconfident in the product, we then need to change what it is that you believe a product is and redefine that. We redefine what a Product is. And then with the sales, when you're uncomfortable with sales, I want to show you a sales process that is going to make sales way more comfortable, way more fun, easier, more repeatable.

Figure 4: People, Product and Process

The way that you want to attract more customers, find more customers, make it compelling for them is first of all, focusing on their problems. Which sounds counter-intuitive. But trust me, when you have a list of a hundred customers problems, and their top three problems, that's when things really begin to change.

Look at how I'm explaining this to you. Top three problems, uninterested customers, unconfident in the product and uncomfortable with sales. We're then going to look at the transformation. This is the transformation that they want to go on. What are they willing to sacrifice? What are they looking to change? What are they willing to change? And then we want to frame it around their future. You're going to hear that word a lot in this book because the future is what it's all about.

12

Sell Futures, Not Features

And we need to start selling the future to our customers. That is the start of creating incredible sales processes and really driving up your revenue. Focusing on their problems, looking at their transformation, and then defining their future.

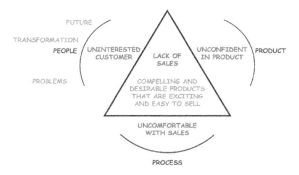

Figure 5: People - Problems, Transformation and Future

A product is not a thing. I think a lot of people think a product is the delivery. It's the Xbox controller or the phone. With services for example people think the service is "accounting". And that's not true. A product is made up of three things. First of all, it is made up of benefits. I've heard it said that a product without benefits is not a product. And that's absolutely true. How often have we seen on Shark Tank and Dragon's Den some widget that someone's created, but no one can quite figure out how it benefits them? They ask questions like "what's the point of it?" And the inventor's response is "no, no, no, this is life-changing, it's revolutionary!" But if other

13

people can't see the benefit in it, it's not a product.

Then we have the offer. The offer is essentially what do they give you and what do you give them? What do they walk away with? How can they buy it? How can they use it? That's getting closer to what the thing is, but it still actually isn't ever "the thing". The Xbox controller, the phone, the accounting, never comes up by the way. That's a delivery method. And we're not going to cover that in this book. And then finally, the message. This is what you tell them. This is how you convey to your audience "this is a product that we want to talk about." People talk about things they're confident in. So this is how you demonstrate confidence in your product, by the message.

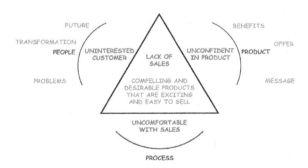

Figure 6: Product - Benefits, Offer and Message

And then finally the sales process. Let's not over-complicate it. The first piece is to qualify, make sure that they're the right customer for you. Not that you're the right product for them, that they're the right customer for you. And next we sell, which is really just a case of taking the problems, the transformation, the future, the benefits of the offer, the message, putting it towards them, asking them the right questions and working out "Is this now the right product for you? Is this the right relationship for us?" Selling is:

1. A transference of enthusiasm and
2. working out with them makes sense for two parties to work together.

That's all it is. And finally the close. That's the part that I think most people need help with. They have these amazing products and offers, but if you're not confident with closing, and if you feel uncomfortable with someone saying "no, I don't want to buy this because"… whatever their reason is, you're going to really struggle to make sales.

Sell Futures, Not Features

Figure 7: Process - Qualify, Sell and Close

So that is the Sell Futures, Not Features, model and methodology. And that's what I'm going to take you through in this book. It's not particularly complicated, but I think it's going to transform your business, if you follow it through.

Do you want more sales?

The question should really be "do you really, really, REALLY want more sales?"

This might sound insane and even obvious. Of course you want more sales, who doesn't want more sales? However having taught and coached sales for a lot of people for a long time, this is often an underlying problem that has a tendency to sabotage our sales driving efforts. I'm a firm believer that the best evidence for where you will go, is looking where you are at. I believe that people are creatures of goal pursuit, meaning they take actions which suit their goals.

This means that if a business is struggling with sales, it's usually because deep down a part of them doesn't want more sales. This is extremely upsetting and even distressing to a lot of people, because of course they want more sales, everyone wants more sales! And if I've written a book about how to get more sales, surely that means that people do struggle with sales.

But the question isn't do you want ANY sales? The question is do you want more sales? Do you really want more

16

customers or do you want better customers? Do you really want more sales or do you want the same number of customers, with higher revenue? Do you want more sales or do you really want more repeat revenue from the same customers? Do you want more sales? Or do you really want more income without risking any more embarrassment, controversy, criticism or aggression?

Every single action I'm going to tell you to take at some point, is going to annoy or upset someone. Is the question really "how do I get more sales without annoying people?" Or "how do I get more sales without potentially embarrassing myself and looking like a pushy second-hand car salesman?" *Chances are, you already know how to get more sales, you're just looking to do it without upsetting people.*

Not many people deep down understand the question that they are asking themselves, when they ask how am I going to get more sales? Human lives and human beings I believe are very simple. However, we have a habit of overcomplicating our own lives for the sake of not offending or upsetting other people. It's extremely simple to generate more sales. The complex part comes when you try to negotiate and navigate the endless feedback, political correctness, criticism, well-wishers, family members, colleagues, previous customers and audience members. Everyone has an opinion and everyone has an agenda. Chances are, you already know how to get more sales, you're just looking to do it without upsetting people.

Deep down most businesses aren't looking for more sales, deep down they're looking for an easier life. Many business owners secretly want to be treated differently. Many of them want special treatment or easier circumstances, or an easier life. Many people take on new training or even entire staff members, only to have to fire them so they can be proven right that "they knew all along that this wouldn't work."

I have repeatedly seen managers and business owners' self-sabotage an expensive hire, because it was obvious to me that their motivation was really to prove that any kind of change or adjustment won't work. Why do they want to prove that something doesn't work? So they can continue feeling sorry for themselves, and play the victim. This might sound delusional or even insane. But it's far more common than people might think. Presumably, you aren't one of those businesses. Presumably you are not one of those people, that looks to play the victim.

Interestingly, the further through this book you read, you'll uncover tools and processes I use to uncover whether your potential customers are one of those victims. Or if they are one of those control freaks, or someone who wants to be proven right.

This might sound sick or even psychopathic. And I would be inclined to agree with you. But it's worth asking the question of yourself, do you want more sales? Or do you want your current lifestyle, just with fewer complications and problems? More sales is about taking on more responsibility. But it can also mean making better decisions with your current lifestyle.

More sales might mean an increase of 10 customers to a hundred within a year, for the same product. Or it might mean 10, $5000 customers turning into 10, $25,000 customers. Before you can continue with this book I need you to be hyper specific and clear on the objective of "making more sales".

This book will help with either of those objectives, or any other goal you might have. Perhaps you're starting from scratch. Perhaps you've been running a business for 20 years and want to reignite your desire to help people. As the subtitle suggests, this book is about taking even the most dull, boring and common services and finding hidden and desirable compelling benefits that are so good you can't help but sell them.

This book is about turning you into an enthusiast and champion for your own products and services. It's also about turning you into a champion and enthusiast for your customers. Because really that's the only thing that matters. Rule one of selling is focus on the customer not the product. And when we discover hidden benefits to our own products, it can be tempting to fall in love with them. Of course, we're taught that it's tacky or gauche to talk about "yourself" and that you shouldn't promote and champion your own products, but I'll take a salesperson who is enthusiastic about their own products any day, over someone who doesn't care about their own products. It's easy to make the transition from caring about your product to caring about the customer. The mistake many businesses make is not being enthusiastic about their product and also not being enthusiastic about their customer. You need to be enthusiastic about both the product and the customer, drawing your enthusiasm about the product from how it will help and benefit the customer.

Before we understand the sales process, we have to really ask ourselves "do I want more sales?" And what we're really asking is "do I want to change?" Not just change for the better but confront some uncomfortable and even upsetting truths in order to change. Overcome awkward and clumsy mistakes and situations to change. Am I ready to change myself, my approach and even my beliefs? The real question isn't "do I want the end result?" The question is "am I willing to put up with the bumpy journey, late starts, dead ends and steep climbs? Am I willing to endure all of that even if I don't change?"

Perhaps this is already deeper than a lot of other sales books you've read. But as you understand the process of sales, you'll understand it affects every single part of your life. Sales has helped me become a more compassionate person. It's helped me become a more contemplative and thoughtful person. It's helped me become more mindful, empathetic, sympathetic and in touch with my emotions. Sales isn't a process of talking the most and the fastest until someone relents. It's about understanding someone's life and offering the best solution available to them. When you answer some of the questions that we'll be asking customers, you'll see how this goes further than basic revenue generation, and deeper into sales philosophy and business wisdom.

So the question we need to ask before we continue is "am I willing to change?" If you are, read on.

Help anyone but not everyone

The immediate and uncomfortable truth you are going to have to tackle head-on, right from the start, is that you can't help everyone. You can help anyone you like, you just can't help everyone. I often find this is the biggest tell as to how committed someone is to the sales process and generating more sales. Lots of people talk about hunting and I've made that mistake in the past. But in retrospect I believe sales is less like hunting and it's closer to animal conservation. I think that working with animals, learning how to conserve them and protect them and educate people on them, is a closer metaphor to sales than hunting them. Partly because most people who hunt African game animals are giant morons. But also, because it's extremely difficult to continue to sell to something once you've killed it.

And just as with conservation, you could help absolutely any animal you want, but you can't help every single one of them. As tragic and heart-breaking as that might be, you are going to have to make a choice. And really, this comes down to a very specific question which people often misread.

Who benefits from your help the most?

What this question means is, which type of customer would benefit from your help the most? NOT who is the loudest and most desperate out of your audience. Neither does it mean who is furthest down the ladder? Some businesses tell sob stories and bleeding-heart narratives in order to get your attention. But just as if you were a doctor and you could see that someone had a head wound compared to someone who had just cut their finger, you'd know who to treat first, it doesn't matter if the person with the cut finger is screaming the most in kicking up the biggest fuss.

"Who benefits from your help the most?", is a question that takes your skills, your interests and passion and combines it with people who will realise the biggest difference. I love the phrase "the gods help those who help themselves". Often characterised by Aesop's Fables and commonly attributed to

Benjamin Franklin as "God helps those who help themselves". It means that if someone is already working toward an objective, they don't have time to play the victim, or tell you their sob story. Someone who is already making sales, would benefit more from this book than someone who runs around circles. Someone who is already making the right decisions will benefit from your work, more so than someone who just wants you to do it for them.

I've talked about defining a niche in my book Five Figure Funnels, and I won't repeat the process here. Even if you are not a marketing agency, I highly recommend reading the first chapter on Audience, in order to better define your ideal niche.

Interestingly, this question also tells me if someone really does want more sales. If someone actively decides that they are going to focus on a very specific customer, that's a good indication that they do genuinely want sales. However if someone's underlying and deeper motivation is to be treated as the victim, or because secretly they see struggle as a virtue, then they won't commit to a niche, audience or ideal customer because they don't really want to find more customers. Ever had a kid struggle to make a decision, because deep down they don't want to do something? It's the same principle.

Again you might question why someone doesn't really want more sales. That's almost irrelevant. The fact is if they don't want more sales deep down, even if they tell people they want more sales, they aren't going to commit to a specific audience. And again, if you find yourself unable to commit to an audience or a specific type of customer, ask yourself why. Why aren't you willing to commit to a customer type? Is it because deep down you feel it's more convenient to live your life as it is now, and struggle through and battle, **because we're taught that struggle is a virtue?** Of course you can change that immediately, and decide that you are willing to change and commit to something specific.

And just with conservation, if you try to help all animals, you won't help any of them. You need to decide if you are going to work with rhinos, elephants, donkeys, exotic birds, fish or any other animal. Because until you've defined exactly who you want to work with, I can't help you go any further. I need to know the exact type of animal that you want to work with, in order for us to discover where to find them. You are going to find it easier to make more sales, and drive more revenue, if you are specific about who you want to work with, and who you want to help.

It's also going to be extremely important during the sales and qualification process, to know that you can't help everyone. At some point you are going to have to make a choice to turn down a potential client. The money might look good, they might even seem desperate for your help. But

24

somewhere there will be something telling you "this sale isn't right for me." Trying to attract everyone and work with everyone will kill your sales chances. If you chase two chickens, you catch neither.

Remember, these kinds of thoughts are more impactful when written down. Make sure to download our entire 9 part roadmap to help you sell futures, not features for free at sellfuturesnotfeatures.com/workbook.

We'll send you the worksheets that accompany this book for free, straight to your email. Plus, you can follow the exercises along in this book and be one of the action takers.

It's not up to you how valuable a product is

This point goes two ways, both in opposite directions. It's almost cliché of an inventor to believe that their product can change the world. You watch programmes like Shark Tank and Dragon's Den and see inventors who have spent tens of thousands or even hundreds of thousands of pounds on their unique invention. They believe it's going to change the world and add massive value to the lives of millions of people. Only for everyone else on the outside to believe that it's a complete waste of time. As the inventor, or entrepreneur or business owner, you don't get to decide how valuable your product is.

And this goes the other way too. There are far too many business owners and entrepreneurs, who are afraid to promote themselves because they don't want to "oversell" their products. You might be afraid of talking about or even selling your product, because you don't want people to think you are arrogant or too proud of your products. But the truth is that you don't get to decide how valuable your products are.

Something I absolutely love about talking to children, is they have absolutely no filter. The child will tell you whether your food is tasty or not. Your customers and the market are exactly the same. If no one likes your products they'll tell you, or they won't buy it at all. Many people would take this as discouraging, but it's evidence that you're moving in the right direction. The worst thing you can do is to shy away from sales, selling and marketing your products, because you're worried about what the perceived reaction will be. You have no idea just how powerful or valuable or useful your products and services are.

You could sell a tiny $50 training product which changes the life of the reader and the customer forever. Yes, some people might not use it and get it. And the majority will probably think it's just fine. But there will be a portion of your customers who couldn't live without your product. It's not arrogant or narcissistic or self-involved to understand that you're providing something valuable to people.

I've had customers provide extremely generous and gushing reviews and testimonials for books, products and training. The idea that I could then stop selling it and decide to take that away from someone becomes quite painful. I completely understand the desire to self-regulate your promotion and telling people "how good something is". But it's not up to you. You don't decide how valuable a product is, your market does.

For example, one of my coaching members told me a story about their small product and how valuable one of their customers found it. They said it literally saved them hundreds of hours of work, gave them the confidence to change their approach and took a load of stress off their shoulder. You might take this stuff for granted, you might think it's obvious. But to some people, your products and services are changing their life for the better. Most of us want to do good and contribute to society. If we are creating products and services which are perceived as valuable, and make people's lives easier or better or more comfortable, that's a pretty good indicator towards community contribution.

I'm a firm believer that happiness is measured in the amount that you contribute to society. It doesn't have to be to millions of people or even thousands. But if you can change the life of a few dozen people and contribute to their life, that is a feeling of contribution. And that is where the healthiest form of happiness comes from.

When you're clear that your products could help other

people and make their life better, it's easier to start being a bit more enthusiastic about it. I believe one of the biggest reasons people struggle to make sales, is because they don't believe in their own products, and they're not enthusiastic about their own products. We'll talk about that later. But if you want to start changing your attitude and sales metrics, being enthusiastic about changing people's lives, and how much their life is better after working with you, is a good place to start.

It's not overstating it to say that your products and services have the opportunity to change people's lives forever, for the better. You are contributing to a wider society and affecting people who you might never meet. It's got nothing to do with you how valuable your products are seen as. I've personally written letters and thanked businesses for seemingly standard or even boring products such as spatulas, waste removal workers and rice cookers because they have made my life so much easier. People are certainly surprised to receive those messages, but to me they have done something extremely valuable and made my life easier.

Is helping someone worth being disliked?

The fear of being disliked by people is, in my opinion, the number one reason why people fail to take action. Or, it's the number one reason that people fear changing at all. Many cultures have a philosophy of "wind your neck in" or not sticking your head above the parapet. Don't get too big for your boots. Know your place, know your station. Remember where you came from. Tall poppy syndrome. These kinds of thoughts often prevent people from taking action, making a change or even doing what they think is right.

The fear of offending people, or being disliked, is also the reason people shy away from selling. I think there are a few reasons why people don't like the idea of selling. First, despite driving the entire economy, sales is seen as something unintelligent or beneath those with education. It's also linked to greed and pushiness and selfishness. Which is interesting because I've worked many different jobs from being a chef to manual labour and I found greedy selfish pushy chefs, waiters, business owners, workers and of course sales people. But I've also found salespeople who are thoughtful, empathetic, hard-working, diligent and caring.

I believe the reason that people inherently don't like "being sold to" or salespeople is because they're worried about buying something and having someone else convince them to buy. They don't like the idea of someone else controlling them. Another reason people don't like salespeople is because they hate to turn down or offend the salesperson by saying no. Which is a bit like saying you have no control over your own finances.

29

Sell Futures, Not Features

Another reason I think people don't like sales and selling is because it's seen as "desperate". Which again, is both hypocritical and bullshit. I've met desperate people in catering, insurance, software, media, art and every other industry. Selling and sales isn't tacky, gauche or bad taste. It's pretty much the entire driving force behind human history. The concept that someone can sell an idea to somebody else and both parties must agree it's the best route, is literally the entire ethos behind human civility and progress.

The question now becomes are you willing to risk being disliked, for the sake of helping someone? Unfortunately despite you and I knowing that sales is not only important, it's vital to both businesses and the human race. We can't control how other people feel about us. And unfortunately no matter how openly ethical, moral and chilled your sales approaches, you are going to attract criticism. No matter what you do, even outside of sales and selling, people are going to dislike you.

If you are hesitating about pitching or publishing a new piece of content, ask yourself why you are hesitant. Is it because you're worried about what others will think? Is it because you're worried about offending someone, maybe even the customer? We must move away from trying to satisfy everyone, by leading the least offensive and least impactful life possible. Towards helping the few, and risking offending the many.

The truth is that you won't offend that many people, 80% of your audience won't even care. 99.9% of the entire population of the planet won't care. They will be completely apathetic to your actions and intentions. But there will be a tiny segment of your audience who dislike you and even hate what you do and what you stand for. However, we must risk that in order to help the portion that does value your help and does want your input.

Abortion, vaccinations and blood transfusions are just some of the medical procedures that most people think are not only lifesavers and necessary for the health and comfort of the entire human race. But should also be considered basic human rights. Many doctors, nurses and consultants must deal with uneducated and ignorant vitriol from thousands of people to potentially save the life of one person. You and I might think it's no one else's business whether they are vaccinated or have an abortion or a blood transfusion. But many people believe that those things are unsafe, "against God" or some other bullshit uneducated opinion. But educated doctors with years of medical training and experience know that saving the lives of the few, or in some cases the many, is worth attracting the disdain of others.

Chances are you're not selling medical procedures. But you will attract dislike. It's just the nature of human beings

31

unfortunately. But if you can make the conscious choice that helping someone and making their life better, is worth attracting occasional criticism, you'll find it much easier to help more people. Every time I send out a sales campaign, I'll probably attract at least one email response telling me that I'm spam, another infomarketer or greedy. But every single time I will also make thousands of dollars in sales and help hundreds or dozens of people at the time. If I listened to the infinitesimally small number of people who don't want me to sell (usually because they don't like the idea of someone succeeding), I would be failing to help dozens of other people. Which I believe to be the more selfish action.

I'm going to push this one step further and even suggest that your customers might dislike you at some point. It's surprising to me how many of my long-term customers and even friends at first openly admitted to not being entirely positive about me. I'm very pro-money, pro-sales and on the surface I can see how people would see me as a selfish bullshit salesperson. I've even had customers get annoyed with me when I refused to back down from selling them something. But I've also had customers thank me for my commitment and refusing to quit on them, and eventually selling the product which has massively helped them.

Going back to the medical analogy imagine breaking your leg, and the doctor telling you everything they'll have to do.

Sell Futures, Not Features

Set the bone, give you painkillers, x-ray, keep you in overnight, hook you up to fluids machine, potentially dress and clean the wound, plaster you up and then potentially have surgery down the line. In a hospital, the doctor knows best. Which is why if you said "no, I don't want you to fix my broken leg", they will push past that and refuse to listen to you. They know better than you. They know it's going to hurt, and they know that you're afraid. They don't quit on you. They will do everything they can to make sure that you get that broken leg fixed. And you object, and you call them names but when it's done you thank them. Parents are exactly the same with their children. They know better.

You, need to know better than your customers. I believe that most people are terrible with money. Therefore, their money is better in my pocket and safer, because I will give them something of value in return. I have seen too many people conned out of thousands of dollars, for low quality products for me to give up.

I understand if this philosophy makes you uncomfortable, and you don't want to embrace this straightaway. But the next time someone says "no" to you, think whether you really know better than them and trust in yourself. Refuse to quit on them and continue working through with them and I promise you, they will thank you for you pushing through. It's worth attracting a little bit of dislike in order to help someone.

Automation cannot replace sales

There's a sales concept called ABS which I've talked about before. It means Anything But Sales. Automation is often used as a replacement for selling and sales and no matter HOW complex and clever the automation, it cannot replace sales. The mistake is that people try to avoid selling and sales as much as possible, and will use "automation" as a way to avoid selling.

What I mean by automation is email marketing, paid social advertising, social posting, link sharing etc. Zapier, IFTTT, ActiveCampaign, MailChimp, Spotify. All these platforms and many many more have automation baked into their service or they ARE automation platforms.

The myth sold to many businesses is that you can either replace or create a sales process from scratch, using automation. An example would be creating a 15-part email autoresponder sequence sent to new leads and hoping that will magically create sales and customers from thin air.

Automation is a tool that should be used to enhance or support the sales process, not replace it. Do I make sales on automation? Absolutely. Have I had to sell manually with meetings, calls, Zoom calls, hundreds of webinars and email exchanges before I could fully automate it? Yes.

It's a bit like nutritional supplements for the gym. There

are cases where people who are performing specific and high-level movements would probably benefit from specialist supplements. But the average gym member is almost certainly not going to benefit from them.

When you start to sell and build a sales process, automation needs to be one of the last thoughts. Because you can't automate what you're not already doing. You can't put sales automation into place where you're not already making sales.

Again that's not to say automation doesn't play a role, of course it does and it's responsible for hundreds of thousands of dollars in sales for myself and my customers. But don't use marketing automation, email autoresponders and follow up campaigns sent on a timer to replace manual outreach and communications. You can't hide from sales. Dread it. Run from it. Destiny arrives all the same. The manual grind and uncomfortable push to sell something IS the sales process. You're still carving steps into the side of the mountain. Only when you get to the top can you install an escalator. What a lot of businesses do is distract themselves with busy work building automations and email campaigns, in order to avoid going out and selling. Make sure that you're not falling in that trap.

Morality of sales

Sell Futures, Not Features

Sales often has a greasy or slippery image associated with it. The con artist in the film is usually a salesperson. The used car salesman is often greedy or just trying to take your money. Popular culture has twisted our view on what the salesperson is, and who they are. Fast talking, Ferrari driving, coffee drinkers like Alex Baldwin's character in Glengarry Glen Ross gives us a sense that the only thing salespeople care about, is money. Old stories of insurance salesmen, kitchenware salespeople and high-pressure door-to-door sales arriving at a town and then leaving when they've gutted it, are how we see a team of salespeople.

Getting the best possible result for someone

As with most words in the English language, the word sales or sell, has many different origins and argued etymological roots. However it's pretty much agreed that it's probably a combination of Nordic language and Latin sel, sala and sal.

In the Roman period soldiers were paid using salt, or salis. This is probably where we get the word "salary" from. Using salt essentially was the salary given to soldiers who are serving their country. The word salt and other old European languages with similar words such as sal and sel, had close ties to the idea of service. While the words "sale" and "sell", now mean to give up something in exchange for money, their roots are heavily tied to the service of an audience or a greater purpose.

The very concept of selling and sales, is about getting the best possible result for someone. As soon as you flip your mindset over to the word service and replace the word "sell" with "service", you begin to change your definition of what it means to sell something. If you have a product that can help someone, or a service that can make someone's life better, would you not argue that it is your moral obligation to get that product or service into the hands of somebody else?

The career of sales was certainly hijacked by people selling products that the world doesn't need. The old West idea of the snake oil salesman, selling concoctions to rid children of tuberculosis, or photocopier salesman in the 1980's selling products that businesses didn't really need, of course have left a blight on the career. It's also a common misconception that all salespeople are motivated by money. Yes, the commission is nice. But I know more salespeople who have left very well paying and high commission sales jobs, because the management or the company wasn't supportive.

What does this tell us? That the service of others, and getting the best possible result for people, is not only more attractive to good salespeople but also more sustainable. When you have a product or service that can make someone's life better, just like the doctor in the example above, our job and even moral imperative is to get that into the hands of other people. Let's say that there are still immoral salespeople willing to make a quick buck out there in the world. You know that their product or service is inferior. Maybe they don't offer support or guarantee. Maybe the quality of the workmanship isn't as solid. Maybe the service is oversold and doesn't deliver the results that the customer expects.

All things being equal, would it not be your moral duty to take money from the hands of your audience and put into your pocket, and deliver them a product or service that will make their life better? Taking money away from immoral salespeople who were delivering a substandard product? It's no different from teaching children to invest money and save money wisely, compared to spending it on things they don't really need. Our job as business owners and salespeople, is to help get the best possible result for someone, using our product or service.

Helping someone make a firm decision

Indecision is probably one of the most common reasons that people's lives never change. Many individuals wish for a better life, can't get over the initial hurdle, fear or even just making a decision. There is so much choice available now, that it has become almost impossible for the average consumer to be sure about their decision. Even before the decision over a selection of products or services, the choice about what to look for in the first place can be overwhelming.

One of the biggest misconceptions about why people don't buy, is not the money, or the price, it's the fear of making the wrong choice. Many people are worried that their decisions are permanent and will affect them for the rest of their life. Even if a product will make someone's life better, make someone's life easier and improve the results they're getting. The mental energy it takes to arrive at a decision is often the reason that people fail to buy.

The meteoric rise of comparison sites proves that people are looking to compare products on a like-for-like basis. YouTube reviews, blog post reviews and entire podcasts dedicated to single lines of products, shows that people want more information. The problem however is that more information, inhibits our ability to make a decision. Often called "analysis paralysis", the phenomena dictates that overwhelming someone with facts and information hurts their chances of buying the right product.

As someone who is dedicated themselves to the service of a particular audience (salesperson), your job is to help your audience make the right decision. It's also helping them make a firm decision. By putting less emphasis and weight on the facts, features and data. Focusing more on that customers life, future and benefits, they will arrive at the decision themselves.

When you can constructively put arguments together and help someone see a better potential life ahead of them, that's when you make a sale.

Taking time to understand their situation, where they want to be and their problems, is in itself an intensive act. I've often had customers say how refreshing and almost therapeutic my discovery sessions are because they learn things about themselves. Because I take the time to learn what they want and need, before making a suggestion, they're more likely to make a firm decision.

If you weren't getting paid, but you took the time to talk someone through their options and explored the best possible decision, and then they confidently took that decision and were happy with their choice, would you consider that a good moral act? Of course you would. Being rewarded for your knowledge, time, patience and process does not make it immoral. What makes it immoral is using cheap and fast sales tactics to trick or force someone into making a purchase. Without listening to their story.

Serving them as best you can

When you've decided on an audience that you want to serve, be it independent bar owners looking to manage staff better, CEOs who want to spend more time with their family, single women who want to travel the world safely, or any other audience. You need to make the conscious decision to

serve   them   as   best   you   can.
Serving an audience as best you can, means putting aside your
fears about rejection, procrastination and perfection. When
you decide that you're going to commit to an audience and try
to make their life better, it's very easy to start getting lost in
plans, strategies and getting your tactics perfect. The best
example I can give for this, is refusing to create and publish
content on a free platform such as YouTube or a blog.

When we serve an audience and we have truly committed
to serving our audience, we don't worry that our YouTube
videos aren't as good as everybody else's. We don't worry that
we might have a few typos or an un-optimised blog post.
Frankly this is staggering that it's even still a debate. I can
tell an enormous amount about a salesperson, or a business
owner, by the amount of free content they're willing to create
and publish and promote.

The first objection given to me when I begin exploring this
idea is "I'm not a writer, I'm not a filmmaker, I wouldn't know
where to start" etc. and as I mentioned, your true commitment
to a cause or audience, means you have to ignore your fears
about what you currently are or are not. The salespeople and
businesses that I have seen grow, compared to those who
stagnate, have one massive difference. The sales team that is
trying to serve their audience as best as they can, and creates
free useful, valuable information and content, will win.

Sell Futures, Not Features

The first thing that people want to blame a lack of sales on, is a lack of leads. People talk about cold calling, advertising and all other methods of attracting interested parties. Many businesses struggle with cash flow and simply don't have the resources to invest in paid lead generation activities. But when we stop thinking about lead generation and start thinking about serving our audience as best we can, you will repeatedly come back to 1 option, create free content.

I've heard every objection in the book. There is literally nothing that you could say now, I haven't heard before or someone else hasn't told me.

- I'm not a good writer
- I'm not confident on camera
- I've never made a video before
- I don't know how to record a podcast
- my spelling is not a great
- I don't know how to help my audience
- I haven't got anything interesting to say
- the market is saturated
- there's too much content out there already
- I don't have time

Every single one of these is an excuse, based around fear. There also is not an industry or product or service in the world that has not benefited from someone producing content for the audience. You don't have to start right now after reading this paragraph, but you do have to accept that serving your audience as best as you can, will help you attract more customers and leads.

And the way that you serve that audience as best you can, is to start producing things that you are not very good at. A productivity software company that I worked with, had a sales team of around 20 people in total, including account managers and internal sales. Two of their sales guys took this information on board and started writing useful content for the audience they were trying to attract. It was originally posted on LinkedIn and yes, the first few posts were too short, too long, had typos, not well formatted, and didn't really garner much   attention. But they just took a common question every single day and wrote a couple of paragraphs about it. Over time they could start referring this content manually, to their customers. It wasn't even that long before their current customers and new leads, asked the same questions. The ability to say "I've written about this let me send you a link", is an instant trust builder.

It is also demonstrating that you are willing to serve that audience without a direct financial gain. As salespeople, sales teams and business owners, we might complain that customers think we are only in it for the money. Then prove them wrong! By creating low quality bad content at the start, within a few months you'll have amassed a library of much better content. Within a year you'll have even better higher quality content and you won't have to manually refer people to it any more.

You'll start attracting your audience who didn't know that you existed previously, to your content. It's not quick, it's not overnight, it's not easy. It requires dedication day in day out. But it is the most solid way of proving that you care about an audience. Serving an audience "as best you can", is a specific turn of phrase. Even when you have no customers, no budget and no following. You're still trying to help people "as best you can".

If you're doing something for the immediate financial gain and reward, you're not serving an audience. If you're only willing to give them a product or service when you deem it perfect, you're not serving them as best you can. By the way, the 2 sales guys who worked with this software company, and created their own content were initially poked fun at. Lots of salespeople thought it was a waste of time to create content for customers that didn't exist. Both of those sales guys have now set up their own company and earn a lot more than the salespeople who refused to start doing it.

Believing in a cause strongly enough to try and convince others

Sell Futures, Not Features

Whenever I tell people that I help businesses and customers with their sales approach, their closes, prospecting etc. A lot of people tell me the same thing "I couldn't possibly do sales". Which is absolute nonsense. Everyone is a salesperson.

When you think about your favourite TV show, movie, book. Whatever piece of content that you consumed and rated 10/10. It could be a blog post, YouTube channel, a film. It doesn't matter, because now I want you to imagine is someone who's never seen it.

Have you had a conversation with someone and they told you they absolutely love a specific genre, or a particular topic or an author, and you ask them "have you seen The Dark Knight?" or "have you read 1984?" When someone tells you that they haven't read or seen something that you absolutely love, but they've given you all the indicators that show they might be interested in something that you love, do you shut up about it?

Of course you don't. You talk to them about how good the book, the film, the TV show, the podcast, the YouTube channel, the blog post, the video game or whatever is. You tell them that if they like superhero films they'll love The Dark Knight. You tell them if they love Aldous Huxley's Brave New World, they'll love Nineteen Eighty-Four.

The same goes for travel destinations, workout types,

45

diets, camera equipment, furniture, art. Anything that people connect to, will create raving fans and people who won't shut up about it. Imagine believing in a cause that really mattered. Perhaps you already do have a cause in mind.

You don't have to have a charitable cause or a typically humanitarian cause, in order to feel strongly about it. There are absolutely people who want to eliminate Third World debt, poverty and malaria. There are organisations dedicated to making the oceans a safer place or making our forests and jungles safer. One of the mistakes people make as they try to choose a cause that they think others will be either impressed by, or more likely to connect with. If you've got absolutely no connection to a cause, it will cause burnout eventually. You'll spend so much energy pretending that you care about something, when you really don't.

That's not to say that genuinely believing in a cause isn't exhausting, but it's exhausting for different reasons. It's still hard work but you're more likely to stick at it, even when you're not being paid (which is a guarantee at some point). When you believe so strongly in a cause such as sales training or physical health or mental health, saving the oceans, saving endangered species, helping emerging countries deal with debt, poverty and slavery. You'll find you won't be able to shut up about it.

One of the core components to overcoming typical selling

fears, is to identify with a cause so deeply, and to understand the root problem is so well, that you don't care when people turn around you and say "no". You'll spend every waking second you have, trying to get the word out and helping people. Let's say for example that you understand and empathise with the struggles faced by C-Level directors of FTSE 500 companies. They don't spend enough time with their family, they might be out of shape, and they want to help the world with their products and services.

Your root understanding of their situation and how their life could be better, means you are more likely to attract them as an audience. It also means you're more likely to attract partnership and supplier opportunities for businesses who also target that market. If you believe that the oceans need to be better looked after, wouldn't it make sense to do everything you can to help companies that also try to achieve that goal? If you have a marketing process that can help plastic free businesses find more customers, doesn't that make it a good moral decision to help those businesses find more customers?

Does it make sense for you to help plastic free businesses take money away from companies that produce a lot of plastic or don't care about the ocean? With the CEO example above, if you can help families spend more time with a loved one, wouldn't you argue that's a morally good thing to do? If that CEO runs a company that helps make small business IT infrastructures safer, doesn't it make more sense to help that CEO do their job as best they can?

The key to believing in a cause that you're willing to push past objections, rejection and apathy, is to understand the consequences of that cause succeeding or failing. When you understand the world is a better place when your cause reaches its goals, or it is a worse place if that cause fails, you are now beginning to serve an audience better than any average salesperson or business.

When you understand those consequences, you can do everything you can to convince other people. You become evangelical about your own position and ideas. You'll attract people who value the same things you do, and they in turn will turn into customers. If you offer them solutions for the cause, to make people's lives better, you'll never be short of customers.

It also transcends sales tactics and skills. Someone talking with passion and enthusiasm is far more likely to make a sale, compared to someone who knows the rules of the game, but has no conviction in what they're saying. One of the first paragraphs of this book talks about how sales is a transference of enthusiasm.

If you can make someone else enthusiastic about your cause, your sales tactics and skills will go much further. So many people are weak at sales because they have no conviction about what it is they're doing. They don't understand how it makes people's lives better so therefore they're non-enthusiastic about it.

When you don't care how your product or service makes people's lives better, you're always going to struggle to make sales. When you understand the consequences of both yourself and your cause succeeding or failing, you don't have time to face rejection or worry about perfection or procrastination, as you know how important it is to get out there.

Expert status and admiration from your audience is not based on being really good at sales or running the best business. It's based on your conviction to further the cause and make people's lives better.

Making a sale benefits the customer

This is probably the most cut and dry argument for why sales are a morally good exercise. When you sell a product or service to a customer that makes their life better, and benefits them, there is a morally good outcome. Absolutely no one can argue with that.

Internally we might have reservations about how much benefit a 4K camera or a brand-new smart phone, or a new Lego set can bring someone. The first thing you must do is to understand that it's absolutely none of your business how a product or service benefits somebody else. If someone feels

49

that a new tripod for their camera, or a new controller for their Xbox makes their life better, who are you to say otherwise?

Consumerism is often blamed for people's unhappiness, depression and feeling a lack of fulfilment. Ever since the enormous rise of social media, many people now blame their lack of happiness, or unfulfillment on seeing other people's lives displayed as perfect through Facebook, Instagram and YouTube. This is not a book about happiness, but I think that most people who are "unhappy" are so because they a) care about what other people think too much and b) don't focus on what they're contributing to society.

I believe the entire purpose of life is to contribute to every other living creature on the planet and make the world a better place. I believe in short, that the meaning of life is to contribute. However you want to define contribution. People who work for 40 hours straight rescuing war children from injuries wouldn't call themselves "happy". People who spend their entire career trying to clean up the oceans I don't think would call themselves happy. There are of course moments of happiness during that period, but what provides happiness is completely different for every single human being, depending on what feels like the greatest contribution to them.

What provides happiness is when someone's life is made better. And if you do believe that consumerism or needlessly spending money on items makes people unhappy, and does make the world a worse place, then you should be taking that money from people and giving them the better option. It's extremely easy to have an indignant argument about selling, marketing, consumerism, without providing alternative.

All of the alternatives we explored that don't rely on service, haven't worked out. If you genuinely believe that people should spend less money on satellite TV, or holidays, fine. But if you believe that strongly about it, you need to have an alternative and serve that audience. You need to get your alternative into the hands of those you wish to serve.

The messy or sickly feeling we have when it comes to making the sale, is rooted in a variety of reasons. Partly because of our beliefs around money, our experiences with salespeople. But many people cringe at the idea of "making a sale" because they don't want to be discovered as a fraud, an impostor or to be seen as taking someone's money. Instead of thinking about taking money from a customer, think about giving them a benefit. Maybe you've got productivity software that allows them to feel less stressed. And they feel less stressed and they sleep better. When they sleep better, they're more likely to engage with their family and community. Think about those benefits and how it makes someone's life better.

Think about the consequences of that person having those benefits in their life. In exchange, they are going to pay you and rightfully so. They can give you money which you can then use to invest in your own business, staff, and your family. Pushing past your fears of rejection or being seen as "pushy", requires you to understand the benefits that you are bringing to the customer. When the customer's life is better, and you can see how their life is better, your care less about your own fears. You don't even have a choice as to whether you should or shouldn't get someone that benefit. If you have the opportunity to make someone's life better, you have a moral obligation to do so.

Making a sale benefits you

Let's look at the most obvious reason to make a sale. It benefits you. You have a better life, if you make a sale. You could almost certainly use the income and it adds to your customer network. More sales can cure a lot of fiscal and business headaches. When you're stressed, because of money or lack of income, closing the sale relieves that stress. If you're confident that you can make sales and generate income, you don't live with as much stress as those that can't make sales. You make better decisions and more long-term plans when you're confident that you can close customers.

You don't have to want a massive house and **garage full of sports cars**. This isn't about becoming a hyper-wealthy person who flaunts excess in a desperate attempt to signal success to others. It's about knowing you can do what you want, with who you want, when you want. It's knowing that you're able to make long-term plans rather than just keeping your head above water. Making the sale, benefits you. It literally makes your life better; however you want to define that. When you're stressed and struggling to keep your head above water, does that sound like a good life? How often have you put off things that you want to do, for yourself, because you're unable to afford it?

Do you want to go to the gym more regularly? See your kids when they get home from school? Go on a decent holiday? Your problem probably isn't expenses, it's income. You're not making the income you need. How often have you felt the cycle of paying off bills and debt with a sale, only to fall back into that cycle later in the year? Money going out isn't the problem. That's always going to happen. The problem is money coming in.

Does being good at sales mean you're better with money? Not necessarily. But it does make it easier to change your money habits when you've got more money to work with. Many philosophers have argued that the first step to changing the world for the better, is to be better yourself.

We can't lead what we don't believe. And what we believe is what we are. The better life and pursuit of a better and fairer world for everyone, starts with yourself. One of the most disgusting traits in modern society revolves around "changing others" before we change ourselves.

Protests, articles, videos and cultures have sprung up all over the world with the sole intent of changing other people's behaviour. Deeper still, these same movements disguise themselves as protests of equality or fair treatment. It's particularly strong around blame and blaming previous actions for the situation people face today. Income and wealth are a classic example. The millennial generation loves to spout how their parents and grandparents' generation ruined the economy. House prices are high, so is food and petrol, rent, bills and all other costs. Comparatively, yes, they are higher as a percentage per salary than they were. But working opportunities, access to information and education, freedom of choice and the speed at which anyone without education or a network can make money, has also drastically increased.

Through all this blame, hardly anyone looks internally and asks, "what can I do better for my own life?" It's easy to look to others to blame, whether they deserve it or not. It's easier to put the responsibility onto others, without asking ourselves "what could I do to make my own life better?"

Ownership of your situation is the most empowering action you can take. Becoming a better person, for yourself, is the first step to making the rest of the world a better place. It also allows you to see that the world isn't in such bad shape.

When you take responsibility for your actions, you see opportunities where there were threats.

It's a shameful and disgraceful thing to see so many people, rise up and demand change of the world around them, when they have no intention to apply that same energy and indignation towards their own actions. Yes, income levels haven't risen to match many first world necessities, such as house ownership. But so what? Will protesting or wallowing in self-pity change that? And no, posting on Reddit and Facebook about how unfair the world is, is not constructive, it's narcissistic.

On the other hand, the speed at which money can be made is exponential. Children can make incomes exceeding their parents with self-branded YouTube content. Laptops and phones have made it possible to connect with customers and people all over the world. The barrier to entry for selling a product has never been easier or cheaper.

Finally, to make a sale is to make two relationships benefit each other. The very act of listening, empathising and coming up with a creative solution isn't just good for the customer. It's good for you. To do good work, is good. As we mentioned before, if you helped someone make a decision that they're happy with, doesn't that make you a good person?

The patience required and the listening skills demonstrated to get someone to buy from you, makes you a better person.

So many salespeople have increased their income, with the same skills that have made them better partners, friends and parents. Learning to listen, helping overcome objections and providing creative solutions makes you a better person just through doing it.

Making a sale benefits your business

Duh? I mean, obvious right?

Selling your products and closing on deals benefits your business. Well, if it was so obvious, more business owners would know that they should prioritise sales and closing. But instead, we don't. We make up excuses and procrastinate around things like branding, building the website, making the logo juuuuust right. This isn't to say that these exercises aren't important, of course they are. But they're not priorities. The cold hard fact is that sales make businesses better. No business in HISTORY has ever created a powerful brand with a few award-winning ads. Why are Apple, Lego and Google massive brands? Because they focused on getting customer money into their accounts.

Selling is what builds businesses. Nothing happens in the world of business until you make a sale. Literally, nothing. If you don't sell, you don't deliver. So many activities disguise themselves as sales-type activities, like designing a logo and brand guidelines. But 99% of the time, it doesn't result in a close. Unless it results in generating income, it's not sales. Your business absolutely must 100% focus on getting customers to see your value and part with their cash.

I can't pay the bills with "beautiful website". I can't pay my mortgage with "award winning brand design". None of that matters unless you have sales and revenue to pay for it. On the surface, sales benefit your business through cash flow. With enough cash flow and margin, you make profit. When your business is profitable, it has money in the bank month over month. Growth follows sales.

But how else does selling and closing benefit your business? First, you're beginning to build a reputation, or you continue to grow a reputation. The funny thing about reputation is that it can't be bought, but it does have to be paid for. You can't "buy" reputation. You can't just spend a ton of money on ads and magically have a reputation. Lots of marketing and advertising businesses want you to think that, but you can't. Instead, if you want to build a reputation, there must be some kind of exchange.

You must make a promise and deliver on it. That's how you build a reputation. And when you have a massive, solid reputation for delivering on your promises, you don't look for leads and customers anymore. They look for you. But you can't buy that reputation. The other person has to give you something. There has to be an EXCHANGE. When you close a customer, they exchange money for your service. Reputation is built when their expectations are met and you deliver what you promise.

If they don't pay or you don't deliver, there is no reputation built. It's one of the biggest reasons to never ever do free work. Because there hasn't been a big enough exchange between parties. Think about this. If you've ever done free work, have they been your biggest champion? Or, is one of your highest paying customers that holds you in high regard? Who do you have a better reputation with? Don't confuse someone who is initially happy with a free service, with someone who has paid and seen results. Your reputation is only built when something is exchanged.

The sale builds income and reputation. But it also benefits the business as it creates momentum and value. Reputation is great, it's the best brand building exercise you can do. But when we make sales, we increase the value of the business compared to other businesses AND it builds momentum that partners, team members and customers can see. When you sell, you are creating movement. Stagnation is when nothing moves, and it kills businesses. Running water doesn't stagnate, just like a business that makes sales. Repeatedly making sales creates momentum and is harder to stop.

Get excited by your customer's life

Sell Futures, Not Features

While your products might not be the most exciting on the market, they are affecting something which customers do care greatly about. Their life. I can understand why people don't want to be enthusiastic or overly excited about insurance products or office data cabling. However, I cannot understand why people refuse to get excited about their customer's lives. An extremely quick method to gaining trust, building rapport and making a sale is to visibly and audibly become excited about your customer's life, future and interests.

Your customers are stressed. They are working hard, worried about the future and probably feel a little underappreciated. Your products and services at the most basic and fundamental level, are designed to make people's lives easier. Your job is to relieve some of that stress and make them feel a little more confident about the future. If you stop thinking about the product for a second, and start thinking about your customers, you'll realise there's a lot to get excited about. When you ask them "what exactly do you want to do in the future?", listen with genuine interest and respond with an enthusiastic and encouraging manner to their ideas. You would be staggered at how effective this very simple listening technique is.

Some of your customers might think that their ideas and dreams are dumb. Some of them might think that most people won't believe their problems are real problems. If you can demonstrate that you not only believe in their dreams, but are enthusiastic about them reaching them, your products will stand out. Even if you're not talking about the products, your enthusiasm for their life will be extremely appealing to them. Your customers goals and their future are extremely personal and important to them. Many salespeople make the mistake of thinking it's important to get excited about the product, and neglect getting excited about the customers life. I know a friend of mine who sells vacations to Disney resorts, and his enthusiasm is so infectious because he gets excited about what you are going to experience. His excitement for the product is born of his excitement for what's going to happen to you.

You might think you only sell insurance or data management. You could be selling more time with the family, financial security or sleeping better at night. "Imagine how good it will feel when…" is an incredibly powerful statement to reframe the product in the mind of the customer. It's much easier to become excited about someone's future and what they'll experience, rather than the bells and whistles of your own product. A piece of advice my Step-Father Chris, who sadly passed away in 2020, gave me, was "if you want to seem like an interesting person, be interested in other people". Show interest and you'll be interesting. Show excitement and you'll be exciting.

No such thing as a quick sale

This is a problem I see come up time and again especially in Facebook groups, forums and YouTube comments. The question of the comment goes something along the lines of this.

"Everyone, I need to increase my revenue by 50% in the next three months, I need to make a lot of money quick. Please help."

It always disheartens me when I see comments like this because typically, they are made by people who are looking for constant quick fixes. It's as if they're constantly looking for the best shortcut to the top but because they have to do it every six months they also end up starting again every six months. I need increase my revenue by 50% in three months

They've probably been doing this for three years looking for six different business ideas or sales tactics or quick sales, they could have been building a really amazing brand that will generate them much more revenue at the same time.

It's time to get this out of the way, this book can't get you a quick sale. There is no such thing as a quick win, or an easy sale that will just magically skip part of the process. There are no special tactics, there are no underground sales techniques. The only thing you can really do is to build a long-term brand, with long-term relationships. I now make more money in sales daily, than I would in an entire month. That's because I've stuck to a sales process, rather than finding the next big thing.

I'm also often staggered by the question of "I need increase my revenue by 50% in three months" or "I need to make a lot of money quickly." Because they usually come with a series of caveats. I can gladly increase your revenue by 50% in the next three months, it's just going to cost you a lot of money to get there. Oh? You don't have any money? Or you don't want to spend any money to generate more sales? Then it isn't your sales process that is broken, it's your business model. Besides, if there was some universal secret method to generating quick easy revenue, wouldn't we all be doing it?

Getting better at sales is about developing better relationships, not finding hidden "growth hacks" to generating quick revenue. Coincidentally you can make quick revenue really easily if you've done everything else in this book. If you've got a compelling offer, you care about your customers and you've built a large audience, it's relatively easy to generate a large income overnight. It just takes a long time to get there. You can't rush history and you can't hurry growth.

If you plant a field of crops and keep asking people "how can I get these crops to grow 50% faster" you're either going to be sold snake oil that just could damage the harvest, or you'll keep pulling up the roots to check on their progress.

You need to let things grow, to have that big payday. And if you put in the time and effort now, you won't have to rely on immediate cash windfalls so much in the future.

Does it make sense for us to work together?

One of the best definitions for "the sales process" that I've been taught is:

> Sales is working out if it makes sense for two parties to work together.

This definition was so clear to me because it immediately helped me visualise being on the same side as the customer. It took all the pressure off the sale and closing, and instead helped me see the sale from the customer's side. Does it make sense for us to work together? This also helped me start to turn down work that I thought wasn't right for me. Either because of the budget, the work itself or the customer. It's not just about you and the productSo therefor, it's not just about the customer, it's about two parties coming together and seeing if they can make something great.

Does it make sense for us to work together? Does the customer have the resources, specific problem, time, budget and attitude to get these results? Do I have the skills, experience, motivation and time to deliver these results? Instead of worrying about proposals, closes and objections, I now try to work out if it makes sense for us to work together.

If it makes sense to me, my job to is to show the customer how much sense it makes. I also began to push past objections when the customer has them, because I knew how much sense it made for us to work together. I wasn't going to throw this away!

Sales is more than just working out what people want, it's helping them find the right solution and in that vein, figure out if you're the right pairing. Does it make sense for us to work together? If you're not right together, it doesn't mean one of you is "wrong" or bad. It just means that you're not compatible this time. I love steak and I love Oreos, but I'm not putting them together anytime soon.

People buy future transformation

The pursuit of superiority is often misunderstood and misused by those that don't fully understand its definition. The truest form of pursuing superiority is superiority over oneself. Especially, one's idea of oneself. It's about bettering yourself and becoming a better version of "you". This desire to improve our sense of worth, identity and superiority is what drives almost all sales. Deep down we make the decision to buy and purchase something because it either supports our idea of who we are (our identity) or our idea of who we want to be (our superiority). While many people might buy a nice car, house, holidays etc. to impress others, either because they consciously want to impress them or be seen to be better than them, it's all tied much deeper to our desire to be a better version of ourselves.

Ultimately people are buying a better future version of themselves. They're buying transformation and superiority. It is a totally illogical and emotional decision. We can fool ourselves into thinking we're rational buyers or "none of that advertising stuff works on me", but all purchases are emotional decisions. We do a really good job of justifying that purchase to ourselves with "logic" (even though true logic doesn't enter the equation ever), asking about cost and features after we have made the decision to buy. And even then, those "logical" questions are internal justifications that we feel other people will ask us. People who we want to impress or we admire or want the approval of.

For example, let's take Sam buying a new marketing project from a consultant like you. You make the pitch, say all the right words and Sam has internally made the decision to buy. She agrees with you that it makes sense for you both to work together. But why is she buying? What reason deep down is her motivation for buying marketing services from you? Here are some of the top-level reasons that seem sensible (logical) to buy from you.

1. Increase the number of leads that the business will generate

2. Increase the number of sales we'll make

3. Increase the number of customers we'll attract

4. Increase the amount that each customer spends

5. Increase our visibility in the marketplace

These reasons could be different depending on your niche or the specifics of your skill set. But these are sensible top-level reasons why someone would buy from you. But almost every single business in the world wants those above 5 bullet points. Why did SAM buy from YOU? Why does Sam want any of those things for her business?

If she generates more leads and sales, her business might grow. Then, she might feel like she's succeeding. Sam begins to feel that she's running a real business, a grownup business. Something she can be proud of. Something she built and contributed to. Deep down her reasons for buying have nothing to do with sales and leads, those are just a means to an end. Sam's real reason for buying is because she wants to BE a success and, in her eyes, that status of "success" comes with certain characteristics. When people ask her why she bought marketing consultation from you, she'll tell them it's because you helped her with leads and sales etc. But the real reason is that she wants to continue her journey towards being a success. She wants to become and transform into a success.

We sell futures, not features.

Sales is a transference of enthusiasm

I just want to end this chapter with another definition of the sales process.

Sales is a transference of enthusiasm

Zig Ziglar

If all else fails, be enthusiastic. Enthusiasm adds about 10 IQ points. Be excited about the product, be eager to learn and listen to the customer. All things being equal, people would rather buy from the person who is energetic, excited, empathetic and eager to help. If two products are exactly the same, same price and same features, the salesperson who smiles and thinks it's a great idea to buy, will make the sale.

If you encourage customers to follow their dreams and goals and agree that their past mistakes weren't their fault and they can change, they'll buy from you. What people are looking for is support and knowing that they're making a good, smart decision. Facts don't' sell, enthusiasm sells. Facts can't make someone think that they're making a smart, rational decision. It sounds counter-intuitive, but everyone who votes believes they're making a smart decision. But absolutely zero of those votes come from a place of logic or rationality. It's an emotional decision won by the enthusiasm of the leader or in the case of voting, the people around you.

"But Mike, you can't just sell on enthusiasm, that's how

people get conned – it's immoral"

I hear all the time, that people don't want to sell with enthusiasm because they see hype marketing and bullshit claims with the same energy all over the place. So therefore, people become confused about the role of energy, excitement and enthusiasm in the sales process. They think that if they act with enthusiasm that they're conning someone or building up the product too much. Or, they're worried that people will think they're a scam.

Being excited about your product has **absolutely zero bearing** on your ability to deliver a great product. Unfortunately, having a great product that does amazing things and delivers amazing results has absolutely zero impact on your ability to be enthusiastic about your product either. Just because you have a good or bad product, that does not affect HOW you should market it. If you really really believe that there are bad products out there that are taking people's money because they market and sell with energy, excitement and enthusiasm, then don't you have a moral obligation to also take that customer's money and deliver a great product? If you really do think that your product is better, then you should do everything you can to take their money and prevent them from spending it on lesser quality or inferior products.

This is why it's so important to ask that first question, do you really want more sales? Do you really truly believe so much in your product that you're willing to risk looking like a crazy person or overly enthusiastic just to get more sales? If you have a true deep conviction, that your solution is the best on the market, you'll become fanatical that people should buy from you. If you're afraid to be proud of the product, it's because you don't believe in it and you don't really want more customers.

People also WON'T think that you're scamming them if you're excited. People that are "scammed" by hype marketing usually don't think they're being scammed at the time, they think they're making a smart decision. Unfortunately, you could deliver the most morally solid, ethical product IN THE WORLD and deliver it with the grace and serenity of Audrey Hepburn, but someone somewhere will think it's a scam. Nothing you can do about that. It's because to those people, it's important that others know how smart and individualistic they are. They love to cry "scam!" at the first instance and tell others so they feel smart. It's got nothing to do with you. So you have two choices.

1. Continue to sell without enthusiasms and let others scam your customers (and some people will still think you're a scam too)

2. Sell WITH enthusiasm and take money away from scammers (and some people will still think you're a scam too)

If you're serious about building your sales process, these kinds of exercises are more impactful when written down. Make sure to download our entire 9 part roadmap to help you sell futures, not features for free at sellfuturesnotfeatures.com/workbook.

We'll send you the worksheets that accompany this book for free, straight to your email. Plus, you can follow the exercises along in this book and be one of the action takers.

Summary:

- Sales is a method of helping people make a decision. You have to be sure that you're helping THEM make the right decision
- Do you want more sales? Or do you really want more income and revenue with less work, and things to not change too much? One of those is more likely to happen and the other is impossible – get clear on if you're really positive that you want more sales
- To grow sales is an exercise in giving up more. Give up being liked, give up following trends and give up selfish pursuits
- Ultimately, we're transferring enthusiasm about something which can help people. Then working out if we're a good fit for each other –

Sell Futures, Not Features

that,   is   selling

Chapter 3 - Creating offers from products

Compelling hidden desirable benefits

"It's not about you"

The Ancient One, Doctor Strange

Product centric to customer centric

Basically, we need to shift the focus of the sale from the product, to the customer. No one buys a bed, a laptop, a holiday or $30 million worth of mining machinery. They buy a better back, a more productive day, memories or the admiration of their boss.

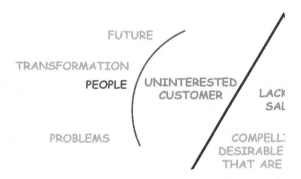

Figure 8: Focus on their Problems, Transformation and Future

People don't buy products; they buy a better future version of themselves. Sell futures, not features. So many businesses get caught up in making their features sound better and bigger and faster. When really it all boils down to how does the customer feel about themselves now, and how will they feel after they buy from us?

Imagine you're broken down at the side of the road and you call roadside assistance. In the UK we have the RAC, AA and a few other breakdown recovery companies, most of whom identify themselves with a bright colour for their van and brand. AA is bright yellow, RAC is orange. When it's pissing down with rain and you're broken down on the M5 outside Bromsgrove, seeing those bright yellow lights coming towards you feels like it's the Avengers coming to rescue you.

So now imagine that the driver hops out, asks what seems to be the problem and after you explain it to him, he asks you to follow him and take a walk back to his van. He slides the door open and starts explaining all of the awesome tools and kit he's got. He goes into great depth explaining every wrench, bit, tool, doodad, thingamajig and wotsit. Clearly, this man loves his job and wants to show you everything he can use and has at his disposal to fix your car. He's doing a really thorough job of explaining the features.

But of course, you don't want to know all that. What you want to know is "when can I get back on the road?" The future version of yourself is one which is driving on the road, safe and warm in your car. Roadside assistance talking about how great their situation is, and all their features, is product centric. You thinking about your car and your situation is customer centric. That's what we mean by customer centric, over product centric.

Many businesses become convinced that they need to educate their customers on features. As if customers knowing what features are better than others, will help them make a rational choice and presumably, the best choice is buying from that particular business. This is especially true of comparative features such as size, weight, price, etc. Laptops compare processor speed, weight and storage. Cars compare MPG and passenger seating. And most service businesses compare price, experience and tools.

All of which are totally nonsensical to understand until you've learned exactly what future the customer is looking to build for themselves. What do they envision themselves doing, seeing, feeling, becoming and eating after buying a product or service, like yours? The features aren't useful unless they're specific to the wants and needs of the customer. I know you'll have heard this over and over, but what it boils down to is that you can pretty much sell anything if you're fully focused on what the customer wants. If you just repeat back to them what they want in their life, you'll be closer to making a sale. Stop selling the tools in the van, start selling "get back on the road". Sell futures, not features.

Sell Futures, Not Features

In this chapter, we're going to shift the focus of your business, products, services and even your brand to becoming more customer centric and less product centric. You'll start defining your business through the market that you serve, rather than the products you sell. Eventually, you'll lean into and heavily promote the emotional, illogical and touchy-feely human side to what you do, rather than the factual features that you have. Features change over time. They evolve, get better and faster and cheaper or disappear altogether. When PCs first started being sold to the public, they were bulky (and sometimes beautifully designed) machines with features like:

- 32mb ram
- 5gb hard disk
- 233mhz processor
- All for £1299!

Source 1: 1997 ad from The Sun. Image taken by zaphad1 on Flickr

Figure 9: An absolute beast. Future-proof.

Your wireless headphones have more power than those PCs back then. The features have moved on and the businesses that have survived the rapid Moore's Law of growth have done so because they've defined themselves by the market that they serve and the goal of that market.

- Seagate – reliable storage
- Dell – reliable computers
- Microsoft – productivity for users
- Apple – art meets technology

Many businesses fall by the wayside because they refuse to focus on the market and customer and instead, focus on the thing that they sell. People aren't loyal. We like to think that as consumers we are loyal, but deep down we're easily swayed and fickle. I'm not so committed to Ask Jeeves that I'll ignore Google when it comes out, just because I've been using it for years. People are not committed or dedicated to features, so stop relying on them for the sale.

The problem is exclusive of the solution

"Oh my God! I absolutely must find a marketing consultant!"

Literally no one in the history of mankind has ever woken up, drenched in sweat, thinking that they need to hire a marketing consultant. No one has ever lost sleep over needing to hire a consultant or needing to buy something.

People are focused on their problems, not your solutions. The problems they are experiencing are a part of their life and those problems exist whether they know about your solution or not. This is perhaps one of the hardest shifts to make in customer centric messaging. It's a paradoxical thought to have, when of course you know that your solution exists. But you need to pretend that it doesn't exist. The customer's problems have got nothing to do with your solution. They're looking to fix a problem or change something and it just so happens that if they learn about your solution, they might be interested.

Customers are way more interested in their problems than

your solution. I once heard an amazing quote from Daniel Priestley saying "you need a PhD in your customer's problems." The reason this is so powerful is because it's not suggesting that you need a PhD in your own solution or method. Above all else, you need to be an expert in your customer's problems. Care about their problems and their life and you won't go far wrong. Instead of marketing your products and solutions, market their problems and their life.

We spend a massive amount of energy telling people how great our solution is and how different and unique it is. Websites, videos, brochures, events, talks, podcasts. All talking about us and our product and services. Instead, every ounce of your marketing, sales and content needs to be promoting and talking about your customers problems and their life. It's remarkably simple and there are only two reasons I can think of that explain why more businesses don't do it.

1. They have no idea/clue about their customer's problems or they don't care.

2. They feel they've invested so much in their clever marketing and slogans that they're worried about scrapping it all in favour of customer centric messaging.

Number 1 is a problem, but not the end of the world. Either find a customer you do care about, or a problem that you have experienced and start getting deep into it. Number 2 is a massive problem because it's usually hinged on the premise that the business owner or marketing manager can't let go of their own ego.

Years ago when I ran a marketing agency, I was so proud of my latest marketing angle and slogan. It was something like "rise up and fight against mediocre design." I had powerful faux-protest signs made and revolution style posters and leaflets made up. I thought I was a creative genius. My ego had totally taken over the project and I insisted this was something that my customers cared about. That was until my mentor asked me "Mike, do your customers really care about the quality of design work out there by other agencies?"

"Of course they do!" I replied, my own ego blinding me to the obvious truth. If they didn't care then why had I just spent a load of time and money on this new campaign? "Have any of your customers ever complained about the design quality of other agencies to you?" He asked.

Slowly, it became apparent that my aim had been off. Rising up against mediocre design wasn't something my audience and customers cared about, it was something I cared about. I was making the assumption that my problems and their problems were the same. I was making the assumption that my solution and their problems were tied together. My mentor asked "what do your customers really worry about?

What are they lying awake at night thinking about?"

The answer was pretty simple "basically, they're worried about being ignored by their customers and being left behind by their competition."

"Right" said Steve (my mentor) "so why isn't your marketing focused on that?"

The moral of the story is that my own investment, energy and time had obscured my vision of the goal. It was a sunk cost fallacy, a cognitive bias that meant the more I invested into the slogans, marketing and message, the better I thought it was. I doubled down and committed to a bad idea, simply because I thought it'd be a waste to not see it through to the end. I was refusing to cut my losses and learn from my mistake and I kept digging deeper. Failing to see that I was going in the complete wrong direction.

Eventually I changed my entire approach and started talking about getting left behind by the competition, being ignored by customers and getting clarity on a plan. It was almost so simple that I couldn't believe it would work, but work it did. I focused all my content, messaging and offer around the problem that the customer was experiencing and it made it 100x easier for them to understand what I did. They knew exactly what their problems were, so I didn't need to explain or educate them. If they weren't worried about attention or getting left behind, fine, I didn't care. I was so focused on who I could help and what their problems were, that I didn't worry if it didn't resonate with everyone.

Stop thinking about your business in terms of the solution you bring to the market. Start defining it by the market you're serving and what their biggest problem is. Your customers are not thinking and worrying and focused on the solution. Amazingly, they're not worried about lead generation, traffic or cashflow management. They're worried about feeling like they're not making progress, or the right choices. They're worried about protecting their wealth for their family (or from their family). They're having sleepless nights over scaling, growing, and sustaining. They're worried that their husband, wife, kids, parents, friends and family are going to be disappointed in them (a staggering number of successful CEOs deep down are afraid that their family don't see them as successful).

Your solution is totally exclusive of their problems. Yes, while your solution might help with their problem, it's not your solution that's going to get their attention and it's certainly not what they're thinking about. They're thinking about themselves and their life.

Don't mention the product

Can you sell something that doesn't exist? Is it possible to sell a product and get someone to buy, without them knowing physically what they're getting? Not only is it possible, it's a vital process in learning how to sell a product at all. Most people make two mistakes when trying to sell anything.

- ⬚ They focus on the product and make the pitch about the thing which they're trying to sell
- ⬚ They believe that the customer just needs more education as to why this is a good product

Customers can't be educated as to whether a product is good or not. Some people will eventually change their mind, but it's a long process. So many businesses try to use facts and statistics to change people's minds about a product or service, failing to realise the facts have never helped anyone sell anything.

A story however, about the customer and how their life will be so much better in the future, is extremely powerful. And in those stories you can sell absolutely anything from coaching to courses to software. Cars, diet plans, marketing strategy, smartphones, office space, asteroid mining. Anything and everything can be sold with a story that doesn't once mention the product or delivery method.

Let me give you an example. I want you to read the copy below and tell me what the product is.

Warning: You'll need to buy an entirely new wardrobe

Customers are furious with us because they've lost so much weight (and kept it off) that they have had to buy a new wardrobe of clothes, because nothing in their old wardrobe fits anymore!

Your friends and family are going to ask what your secret istell me what they product is. In fact, it's going to become a regular part of your daily routine to explain your transformation. How come you've got so much energy now? How come you look so good? Why do you sleep so well? It'll be up to you if you tell them the truth of course!

Imagine being able to still eat your favourite food, lose weight and get fitter in the process. No diets, no pills, no awful machinery. And best of all, it's so simple that anyone can do it. No tricks or fads. Just better sleep, less fat and more energy. Doesn't that sound better? Don't you deserve a healthier happier life?

Now I'd like you to try and tell me what the product is. What exactly is that copy selling? It could be a personal trainer, a gym membership, a home workout course, exercise equipment, a cookbook, a meal plan, classes, surgical procedure or an app. There is absolutely no mention of the product or the method of delivering the results. Which is why I always say results ≠ delivery. The method that you use to deliver results is not the only method

for delivering those results.

And in that copy above, we've focused exclusively on results. No delivery method whatsoever. No features, only futures. And did that copy work? Of course. It was one of the best converting newspaper adverts of all time, offering a home workout course and meal plan. But the point is that you don't need to rely on educating or explaining the features to make a sale. If anything, that could well be harming your sales. Instead, try to sell the product without mentioning the product. You'll need to make the copy entirely about the customer and their life. You could throw in some awards or years of experience, but the bulk will be based around the customer and their life. What they think of themselves and what they want. And you can absolutely categorically do this for every product and service in the world. It might not be easy and the ideas might not come quickly, but they will get there if you give them time and work on it.

Features vs. benefits

If you're ever looking for a solid and quick definition of what a feature is, so you can recognise them, I use the below:

A feature is something which when described can easily be replaced by another tool, competitor or product.

For example, a car is a feature. It can be replaced by a bus, train, plane, bike or

walking. It can also be replaced by other cars. The delivery is exclusive of the result. Results ≠ delivery. A car (the delivery) is not the only method of delivering the results (getting to another location).

A benefit can typically be summed up as "in the future I want to…" i.e. I want to get to work in the morning cheaply and easily. I want to leave at my convenience and listen to my music in the morning."

A benefit is less easily replaced. If someone came up to you and said "hey, I know you like to watch whatever you want on TV, whenever you want. But what if instead you had to stick to a program schedule and could only watch what we chose?" what would you say?

You can't easily replace convenience and choice, because those are benefits.

Electric windows aren't the only method to keep you cool in the car. A Yeti tumbler isn't the only method of keeping your drink hot. A Microsoft Surface isn't the only laptop on the planet. However, hardly anything else is going to make you feel like a success and a bigshot than driving around in your brand new Merc. No one is going to know just how tough and serious you are unless you've got a Yeti. And you want people to comment on your "out the box thinking" and different choice for choosing a laptop that isn't an Apple.

We'll explore more benefits later, but when you're getting into this practice it can seem like there is a blurred line between benefits and features. And there are to some extent. However hopefully the title of this book "Futures not features" highlights just what a benefit really is.

A benefit is just a better version of a future that someone wants. It's the future fantasy which someone is working towards or hoping to buy. A benefit is just a better version of themselves, in the future.

Who benefits? Who suffers?

Imagine if you didn't sell your product and just stopped. To begin understanding how to start selling futures and stop selling features, we need to do a little creative writing and start imagining the consequences of our actions. Deeper impacts to our products that we're not aware of at the moment. In my book Five Figure Funnels I briefly touch on the process of writing out who benefits and who suffers? If you make the sale, who benefits? WHO is a more important question than "WHAT is the benefit?" because it ties the benefit to a human being and a life that has meaning. When we just state what the benefit is i.e. more sales, lose weight, confidence etc. We're still not focusing on who the customer is.

"Who benefits?" asks us who that person is and why

they'd even want that benefit. Does a new business owner want more sales? Does a new grandparent want to lose weight? Does that person want to be more confident? Most people tend to want similar things, freedom, fewer money worries, security, confidence, acceptance etc. Which is why connecting it to the person and a human is so powerful because it puts a face to the impact.

If you make the sale, outside of you, who benefits? The customer of course, obviously. But who else? The customer's family? Their friends? If you're selling marketing strategy consulting, and the customer who buys starts to feel more confident about the direction on their business, that's going to impact home life. How about your bank? At least the call centre staff who have to call you up, telling you that you're overdrawn, don't need to worry about making an awkward call to you now. Because you made the sale. What about the customer's customers? They're more likely to experience the results and benefits of your customer, because you've helped them get exposure or acquire more audience. It scales further that you can see now. Local schools, hospitals and other public services benefit because you'll pay tax and that goes to them. Local businesses and other suppliers benefit because you'll spend money with them. It goes on and on. And that list is so important to have written out because it shows a deeper impact with your sales and your decisions.

And who suffers? If you didn't make the sale, whose life is worse off because of that? Yours, of course, and the customer (or non-customer) in this sense. But the customer's customer suffers. Their family and friends suffer. Their suppliers suffer. Your local school and hospitals, and their local schools and hospitals suffer. There is absolute real pain associated with every non-closure of a deal outside of your own. And I suppose that's the entire point of this book. It's not about you.

If you'd like prompts and reminders on what to write down, head over to sellfuturesnotfeatures.com/workbook and get our Customer Transformation Cheatsheet to help you uncover hidden, desirable benefits.

We'll send you the worksheets that accompany this book for free, straight to your email. Plus, you can follow the exercises along in this book and start your journey to sell futures, not features.

What is their average day?

In order to better sell your products you need to understand what your customers are going through on a daily basis. Customers are looking to change their lives, and this means their daily life. If you can understand what their life is like day to day, you'll have a better understanding of the transformation that they are seeking.

What you're looking to do, is take someone from a life that they want to change, to a better future version of their life.

Sell Futures, Not Features

The trials and tribulations of life aren't summed up in massive life changing experiences, they're shown in the moment-to-moment experiences that someone faces.

One of my favourite exercises is imagining the average day of my customer and thinking how I could make that day better. This is important to do and very powerful because it begins to remove the sales process away from pushing a product and feature set, towards being an attractive offer.

We all supposedly hate those product infomercials where the housewife opens the kitchen cupboard door and all the Tupperware flies out. Or the guy playing golf can't seem to hit a straight drive. And asks a question like "is this you?" While the acting might be bad and the consequences dramatised and exaggerated, the methodology behind showing that you understand someone's life, is extremely sound.

What those types of adverts do is demonstrate a really clear knowledge of the problems that the customer is likely to go through. We can extrapolate further by taking **significant and specific moments** in someone's day-to-day life, and see how it affects their mood, what their friends and family think about them when it happens, what their own self-esteem is with that issue. If you discover why something is a problem for someone, you'll probably uncover a deeper motivation.

Our job is to paint that picture of a better future, which is why I like to look at what their average day is before using your product and after using your product. Think about their average day to day activities. They wake up, have breakfast, head to the gym maybe. What are some of the significant moments in their average day? Before working with you, do they always get to have breakfast with their kids, do they have to get to the office early? Before working with you are they excited to check their emails, or would they dread seeing another empty inbox?

To better sell products and convert a feature set into desirable and compelling benefits, we need to position it from the customers standpoint. And the easiest way to do that is by looking at their average day.

- ☐ List out their average activities
- ☐ Explain what happens before you work with them, during that activity or moment
- ☐ Explain what happens after you work with them during the activity or moment

Let me give you an example. Regardless of what the product is, whether we are a gym membership or a yoga mat, we need to know who our purchaser is, and in this case it's a busy mum. One of the things that might happen in her average day is playing with her kids after school.

So the average activity or moment in this case, is playing with the kids after school. We want to imagine what that activity is like for our mum. In this case we are targeting

90

overweight or out of shape mothers who don't have the time freedom to be able to go to the gym. Before working with us or buying our products, she gets easily tired playing with her kids, but she sees other mums and dads happily playing with their kids without stopping. Before working with us she can only play with her kids for a few minutes before needing to take a break and sit down on the park bench. She feels she is missing out on treasured experiences and feels self-conscious about letting her children play by themselves.

After working with us or buying our products our mum has more energy. Not just because she's lost weight, but also she is sleeping better and enjoys playing with her children more. Now she can lift them up and swing them round and hold them in her arms without needing to take a break. She's building valuable and unique memories with her family that she knows will last forever, long after the children have grown up.

Notice how we don't mention what the product is, or more traditionally what the benefit to the product is. Many people get confused about what a benefit is compared to a feature or a product. They try to frame a feature by over complicating it and saying it's a benefit. In this case we have explicitly stated that the benefit is entirely the perspective of the customer. You can clearly visualise the activity with the children and imagine what it's like to have to take a break. We haven't mentioned whether the product is a diet program, calorie app, exercise program or home exercise course. Because the product and delivery method are irrelevant.

Instead when we start framing the benefits from the perspective of the customer, in this case imagining the future that our mum will experience, they start to buy into a better version of themselves. The customer starts to buy the better future, rather than your product. It just so happens that your product is one of the best or fastest or easiest methods to get to that future.

It's unlikely that you provide a product or service which is so unique that it can deliver a future which no other product or service on the planet can't also do. When you begin to strip away what makes up most products and services, they pretty much are all designed to make people's lives easier or more exciting or fulfil a deeper motivation. However this is also a massive advantage for businesses that do offer similar services.

Many businesses struggle to generate leads and sales because according to them, there is too much competition. Everyone from construction companies to consultants compete for the attention of their customers, by telling them how great they are. Businesses that really flourish, especially in a competitive and crowded market, do so because all of their communication and marketing is from the perspective of the customer. Large insurance companies are often very good at this, even though the service they provide can pretty much be done by an Excel spreadsheet, they heavily lean in to the happy and secure family future angle. They understand they don't sell insurance, they are selling certainty. Just as the same with our new mum in the example previously, we aren't selling her a diet plan or a weight loss program, we are selling her memories with her children.

If you've ever wondered how companies begin to understand "we don't sell "Product" we sell security / certainty/ motivation/health/community etc." it's because they have framed the sales process from the future that it delivers to the customer.

Make a list of their activities

Start by making a list of all of the activities, moments, tasks and parts of your customers day. Here are some examples:

- waking up
- having breakfast
- saying good morning to their partner
- going for a run/going to the gym
- driving to work
- getting the kids ready for school
- cleaning the house
- meeting friends for coffee

- getting to the office
- opening their emails for the first time
- checking their phone
- watching TV
- meeting with the customer
- meeting with their parents
- going shopping for groceries
- afterwork drinks
- going for lunch
- making lunch at home
- picking up the kids from school
- driving home
- having dinner
- checking emails before bed
- checking Facebook
- creating a YouTube video
- going to sleep

As you can see this isn't even an exhaustive list, but if you can create a list of between 10 and 15 activities which your customers face on an average day, you will have a fantastic start for your new future and benefit focused product.

What is that moment like before working with you?

Next up we need to write a short sentence about each moment, before working with you. This is why I believe creative writing is such an important and powerful skill to have. If you can imagine what it's like to be your customer, and put yourself in their shoes, you'll have no trouble making sales. You'll also have no problem discovering hidden, compelling and powerful benefits which people want to buy.

The reason benefits are considered hidden, despite the fact that they could be so powerful, is because so many businesses still insist on comparing their product to other products, or talking about why their products are so great. A really good example of this in recent marketing is the launch of the new generation of game consoles. From memory Microsoft and PlayStation for the new Xbox series X and PS 5, are promoting how many teraflops their consoles can process. I've built my own gaming PC and worked in a large number of tech corporations and I haven't got a god damn clue what a teraflop of processing power is.

From my basic understanding it means that the consoles can do more, perform more and create better looking graphics. As well as essentially process more stuff. But it's like saying "this bathroom has 15 flumpkins, compared to our other competitors bathroom which only has 12 flumpkins." What the hell is a flumpkins?

Businesses then become confused about why the customer is confused. And they start going down a path of educating customers about what a flumpkin is. When you are selling to a customer and you have to explain why a feature is good or powerful, you are missing the point. Educating customers on what a teraflop or a flumpkin is, isn't going to make sales, because it's without context.

If instead PlayStation and Microsoft told a story about the average user experience with a game console and why their console is so much better, such as lightning fast load times, play more games online more often and easily join your friends, then that's appealing.

For example, "with the Xbox one and Xbox 360 if you want to stop gaming for a while or change games, you had to save the game, exit, swap in a new disc, or load up a new application. During this time your Internet connection might become disabled or disrupted. It's also extremely limiting the number of activities you can do with a friend or during co-op and online play. With the new generation of games consoles, you'll be able to seamlessly switch between games without having to load up a new application or even having to pause the game and save. You can quickly switch between different games and continue playing the ones that you want all with graphics that are so good Hollywood is now using them on film sets, rather than rendering them from scratch in a studio. We've reached the stage where games are now so lifelike and yet you can seamlessly switch between them without pausing or even turning off the console, and this is because of the processing power measured in teraflops."

Sell Futures, Not Features

Marketing businesses, accountancy's, consultancies, engineering companies, food manufacturers, education companies, architects and every other industry has a habit of over complicating the sales messaging when the customer becomes confused. If the customer doesn't immediately understand the benefits of a feature or a product, don't continue to over explain the feature, bring it back to their life. After mentioning a product or a feature if the first word isn't "imagine", then you're probably going further into the details. It's like someone who tries to talk their way out of a bad joke by explaining the joke. If they didn't find it funny, because the joke wasn't funny, explaining it doesn't make it funnier.

What is their life like after working with you?

This is now where we can start to explore more creative writing and ask ourselves, what will the customers life be like after working with us? How will their life be easier? How will they feel about themselves? How will other people see them? These types of questions will uncover what your customers are truly buying, and what you are truly selling.

A lot of marketing and sales books talk about the custom avatar. While I believe they have their place, I personally feel that the average day before/after exercise and the following exercise of Compelling Benefits is in fact a better measure of who a customer is. It's extremely important to know your customer's average education, their political leanings, type of content they read etc. But if you can understand what their average day is like and the things they dread and the things they look forward to, you'll have a better insight into their buying process than any of your competitors.

This works for a variety of reasons. First of all if you create marketing and sales collateral focused on your customers, they can now spend more time with their kids in the morning, and no one buys or is even interested, it's clear that they are not interested in solving that problem. Spending more time with their kids in the morning at breakfast time obviously isn't a big pain point for them. This is good news, because you're learning what your customers will or won't buy. So many businesses make the presumption that "of course someone wants to spend more time with their children, that's the main benefit I bring and therefore everyone should want it". But if you don't have kids then it's of little to no motivation.

Instead if you flip it and talk about how "in the future with the next customer meeting, their sales manager will congratulate them and applaud them on their initiative", that might well be the thing that makes the sale. "Our name is Calendar Excellence Consultancy, we work with young executive professionals looking to take their career to the next level. After working with us, at your next sales meeting, your sales manager will not only be impressed by your attitude but will be more likely to offer you a promotion in future." That's a sales hook which if your customer cares about, they'll be interested in. We haven't told them what the product is, we haven't told them what the method is, we are only using the potential desired future as a sales hook. If that one becomes more popular than having breakfast with your kids, you know that what they're actually buying is approval from management, rather than building memories with their children. This either tells you that you have got your customer type incorrect, or your customers don't care as much about one topic as you thought they did.

Again a lot of businesses get this part wrong and they think that customers don't care about one feature over another. If you try to sell a product with 10 flumpkins or 12 Tflop and no one cares, people will try and switch the feature set or, as we mentioned before, go into more detail on that feature set. Instead, you need to start producing sales and marketing collateral around the future which you'll be providing.

Your job is to take your customers from A to Z. It's a journey and where they are now is A. They're experiencing problems. There are things they want to fix in their life and there are things they want to keep. There are things they're afraid of losing and there are things that they are afraid of happening to them. If they want to get to the better future, or the promised lands, or the letter Z, those desired end goals are what motivates them. They want to buy that end goal. They want to buy that future, which is what you should be selling them.

Compelling benefits

If we've looked at parts of their day and wondered what would be better and what could change, we now want to look at what exactly is changing.

In our earlier example we saw a young new mum struggling to play with her kids. She got tired easily and couldn't play with her kids. The question is why does that matter to her? Who cares that she can't play and gets tired? The answer is that she cares. She cares deeply because of her beliefs and internal dialogue.

"You really should be able to play longer you know. There are older parents all around you and they don't need to take a break. What kind of a mother doesn't play with her children when they finish school? You're so tired all the time, wouldn't it be great if you didn't feel tired? What are the other parents thinking about you if you're sat down while they play?"

This internal dialogue is powered by what she sees around her and what she feels inside. What we've done is identify a moment in her day which she would like to fix, we now want to look at lots of different angles to determine what aspects of her day she wants to change.

This is where we discover deep hidden benefits to your products and services. Hopefully you're beginning to see that the product and the benefits have NOTHING to do with you. It's all about the customer, it's all about their life. You might believe that the best thing about your products is the Tflops or doodads or flumpkins. But it's not. The best thing about your products is what they do for other people.

Remember in our previous sales copy example, where we sold the idea that you'd need new clothes and you'd have more energy? Those are hidden benefits that only came to the surface when we dug past the features into the life of the customer and looked at what our features could unlock in their life.

We want to frame our benefits in terms of "before working with you" and "after working with you". It could be purchasing the product, joining the membership, signing up. The method of buying doesn't matter, we're just focused on their life.

Just before we get into the examples list, I want to offer one final model to help you understand what we're trying to do here. Your customers have a "vision" for their perfect life. At least, they have a vision for what a perfect day would be. While it might not be so concrete that they've got it written down (although many do), they have an idea of what they want to be different or better in their life.

Your product's benefits need to match their vision for their life. If one person has the vision that they're able to work 4 days a week and spend the rest of their time hiking, your product needs to help them reach that vision. It almost doesn't matter what the product is, as long as you can comfortably and truthfully say that one of the benefits either gets them closer to their vision or even gets them there completely. It doesn't matter how good your product is, if you can't clearly articulate a benefit that gets them closer to their goals and vision, they won't be interested.

A mistake I see many business owners make is making the assumption that their benefits are universal. That their products help people do X Y and Z and surely everyone would want to have those benefits? It's a dangerous assumption because not all people DO want the same thing. And thank goodness they don't! What a boring world it would be if we all wanted the same thing. You have to match your benefits to the vision of the customer and focus on that. It's very expensive and takes a long time to educate people as to why they should want a benefit.

With that, let's go through this list of prompts for building compelling, desirable benefits that right now, might be hidden in your products. I want you to use fill in the blanks for this sentence:

Sell Futures, Not Features

"Before working with me, my customers [problem]. After working with me my customers [benefit]."

For example, before working with me my customers have zero spare time to spend with family. After working with me, my customers have as much spare time as they want."

Have

To have or not have something is the easiest benefit to build, because it's the most basic. Frankly, most people use this benefit and then dust their hands in completion. If you sell websites, before working with you the customer doesn't have a website. After working with you, they do have a website.

Delving a little deeper, that particular "benefit" was more of a feature. Because it was the deliverable – the website. We also want to look at what the customer has after getting that feature. The future that someone is looking to achieve or realise with that purchase.

Every product is a gateway to something deeper. Older men buy sports cars to recapture their youth (or live a youth they never had). People buy diet books and meals and plans to lose weight so they can feel more happy with their body. Students buy alcohol in a vain attempt to increase their confidence and feel like they have a better chance with people at a club.

Your customers want to have something. Something they don't have now, or something they don't have enough of.

Your product needs to give them a path to that thing. Something which they want to have.

See

What do your customers want to see in their future? What are they seeing now, or what do they see which they would want to change? It's a broad question for sure, but it's a powerful motivator and benefit builder.

People often use the sentence "I just see so many…" or "I just want to see if…" It doesn't have to be a literal sight, although it can be. We want to make a vision come true. Seeing a vision come to life is an extremely powerful benefit.

1) I see my kids' faces disappointed when I have to work during the holidays

2) I just want to see my kids during the week and weekends without checking my phone

If you can articulate what your customers see now, and what they want to see in the future, you'll have an easier time selling your products and service to them. Try finishing off some of the sentences below.

1. Every day when I drive to work I see…(people in nicer cars, how early I have to leave, more and more traffic)

2. When I open my emails I see…(more complaints, zero leads, more admin work)

3. Each time I get to the office I see…(more bills, the

same faces and zero motivation, my idiot boss with a bigger office than me)

4.   When on holiday I see…(loads of couples having fun, young families, people spending money)

You want to try and ask your customers what they're seeing now, and what they want to see in the future. It's a broad question as I mentioned. Some people might want to see The All Blacks win another world cup, some people might want to see the actual winning match as it happens. Some people want to see Venice before it sinks. Others want to see a 15% increase in revenue.

What customers want to see is where they want to go. If your product helps them see a future that they want, they'll buy from you no problem.

Feel

You might already be noticing a pattern here too. I've written the word feel a lot or alluded to it, because every single benefit on the planet is tied to an illogical, emotional desire. The desire to change how we feel.

No matter how stoic, how logical or cold a person claims to be. Every single time they purchase something, it is an emotional decision. Sure, when they tell you why they bought a new sports car, they'll tell you it's because they felt they deserved it or it was a really good price and a good time to buy (all logical reasons). But deep down the reason they bought it is because they wanted to feel something.

Last year I bought a new electric shower. I was standing in the shower and our old one exploded and sprayed super-heated steam right at face level – luckily I had just stepped out of the shower and saw this happen from a distance.

I immediately went onto YouTube and searched if I, a regular non-electrician, non-plumber could replace an electric shower. Turns out I could. So I ordered one via click-and-collect, hopped in the car and bought one that was on sale. £200 and 20 minutes later I had installed a new shower.

You might argue that I HAD to buy a shower. I was replacing a feature which had broken so of course I had to get one. Who doesn't have a shower in their house?! And that's exactly my point. On the surface it looks like I had to buy a shower to replace my old shower. But really, if we dig a little deeper, it's because I felt we HAD to have a shower in the house.

What kind of a husband can't provide a basic shower for his wife and home? What kind of person doesn't have a shower at home? How could anyone take me seriously or even respect us if I couldn't install a shower?

See what happened? The initial logical responses I gave are about replacing something which broke. But deeper down it turns out the real reason I bought a new shower was to show Olivia (my wife) and her family that I can take care of her.

This is ignoring the other massive benefit of having a hot, reliable shower when I've finished work. The cold brutal reality is that our bath, even with a cold shower, is perfectly capable of washing me. Soap and shampoo don't require hot water to activate and if anything, studies have shown that having hot showers can strip the skin of essential oils and contribute to spots and even acne.

The cold logical fact of the matter is I didn't need a fancy new shower, I didn't even really need a new shower. But I wanted to feel comfortable and frankly pampered (it's worth noting at this point that electric showers have come on a LONG way recently and if anything, have some advantages or even benefits over a plumbed in shower).

People who claim to be logic based or only deal in facts are just as emotional as anyone else. They're just better at rationalising their decisions to themselves. True logos and the ability to "think logically" is a paradox and humans aren't good at it. We can repeatedly demonstrate this over and over too.

Think about someone who claims to think logically about all their decisions. Have you ever seen them get upset or emotional? Have you even seen them act stubbornly even in the face of facts? Of course you have, we all have. This is absolute definitive proof that logic doesn't exist in human decision making, rather emotion does and afterwards we work on rationalising it.

How a customer feels before and after working with you, in my opinion, is the single most important aspect of your product and service. The "feeling" benefits are the ones that matter, because feelings matter.

Feelings of security, faith, trust, confidence, happiness, excitement, enthusiasm, accomplishment, success, comfort, relief and many many more are what drive every sale on the planet. People don't buy phones for the processor or the camera, they buy them for the feeling of connection and being on the cutting edge of technology.

People don't buy food for the same reason. Every restaurant, shop and grocer sells food which appeals to different feelings. And more often than not, we can heavily lean into those feelings and begin to build an extremely strong brand.

Before working with me, my customer feels…(unconfident, confused, scared, stressed). After working with me they feel (confident, clear, proud, focused).

The reason I love focusing on feelings is because they're so easy to connect to.

"Do you constantly feel stressed every time you open your laptop? Are you worried about the next 3 months of your mortgage? How are you going to pay it? Will the rates go up? It's a non-stop barrage of confusing and irritating events that never seems to end. When you wake up, do you dread heading into work? All of this can go away – it's just a question of how quickly."

These are hooks and magnets that draw customers to you. We all internally experience our emotions all the time. Some are more common and easier to identify. But we do all run through a series of emotions day in and day out. When a company starts to focus on us and our emotions and feelings, it makes them look psychic. Almost like they can read our minds.

Instead, the company just understands what we're going though, and that we can help. When you start getting specific you build a really REALLY powerful series of benefits (and again, watch how I never mention what the product is).

"Every time you get a reminder email from your bank, how does that make you feel? Stressed? Anxious? Worried? What are they looking for now? Does your laptop now seem like a briefcase full of bad news? You'd rather just ignore it and hope it all goes away. Worst of all, your situation seems so dire that surely no-one could help. You're alone, embarrassed and confused about what to get started on. You know you need to do something, but what?"

Now let's start to build a better future.

"How about feeling in control from today, onwards, forever. Never letting doubt or fear creep into your brain. Do you want a feeling of "I got this!"? How about when you wake up, instead of hitting the snooze button, you step out of bed and know that it's going to be yours for the taking. Confidence with money and spending is within your grasp. It's so close you can taste it."

Feelings, emotions, irrational and illogical thoughts. All of the above is designed to show empathy and understanding with the customer. I still haven't even told you what we're selling, but I can assure you that it's something that people want. Because it speaks to who they are as a person.

Ask yourself what customers feel before, and after working with you.

Eat

The food we eat is a really good example of what we think of ourselves. People who value their cars use premium petrol. People who value themselves, eat better quality food. It's also a good indicator of times of the day and what our priorities are.

For example, if you saw a family heading out to breakfast together as a group and sitting down at 9am for something to eat, in a nice restaurant, what conclusions could you make?

Perhaps they're on holiday, or perhaps the parents have got the day off? Maybe the parents have their working life figured out enough to take the morning off and spend it with their kids? When was the last time you took the morning off to have coffee and a pastry with your partner, or family, or parents?

Flip that and imagine a woman hurriedly walking down the street. She's clutching her bag and trying to get her phone out of her pocket. She just manages to catch the bus to work, drawing up a nice sweat to sit in while she commutes to the office. In her bag she pulls out a small breakfast bar. You know the ones. Marketed as "healthy" but really it's just a chocolate bar with some sugary-fruit in it.

Does that seem like the type of meal that people want? Does that seem like the type of breakfast that most people have?

Taking time to enjoy food is one of life's great pleasures. Olivia, my wife, showed me just what I was missing out on when I moved back to Devon. I personally had survived on beer, coffee and cigarettes (as well as a few other chemicals) before sometimes eating a breakfast bap or a late-night chicken burger. Let this be a lesson to you – most chefs don't eat well.

The way that Olivia convinced me to move to where we are now, was to take me to different restaurants and shops and show me what we could be eating every week or even, every day. Fresh cheese and ham. Local meats and seasonal vegetables. Bread made that morning. Local bakery brownies the size of a laptop. Homemade pasta, sauces, fresh eggs, apple juice, coffee on the beach on a Sunday morning. I was sold.

If your product helps people make money, it helps them eat better. If you help them live a healthier life, then food will be a big part of that. If you help them with their relationships, frame it around food and mealtimes. If they want to travel, get some food in there.

Show me someone's shopping trolly and I can pretty much tell you everything you need to know about them. You can tell a LOT about what someone orders off a menu or where they decide to eat.

Before working with you, what do they eat in the morning? How do they eat breakfast? Who do they eat it with? Who do they want to eat breakfast with? What do they want to eat? If you can give people the time and ability and freedom to eat what they want, with who they want, you'll be closer to a sale.

If I was selling houses, I'd talk about the meals that their family will enjoy. I'd talk about barbeques outside and coffee on a Sunday in the conservatory. If I was selling accounting, I'd sell a stress-free breakfast with the kids knowing you can take a day off to spend with your partner, going and having lunch. If I was selling mobile phones, I'd talk about finding the recipes for your favourite pastry or making amazing memories with friends over drinks.

Do

What do your customers want to do, after working with you? What does working with you enable them or empower them to do? What do they get to stop doing? What are they doing now, that they want more of? What are they not doing now, which they want to?

Doing things can be broken up into the five basic areas of a niche. Wealth, health, relationships, hobbies and status. People want to do more of what they want, when they want, how they want and with who they want.

Sometimes the answer is super basic. "I don't get enough time on my boat and I want to do more sailing."

Some doing activities are not the end result, but a stepping stone. "I want to do more public speaking and paid talking events. I'm not doing enough right now but I feel that'll help me get to the next level."

If you can figure out what people want to do more of, or less of, you'll have a solid hook and benefit for your product or service.

Know

Knowledge is a form of security. While some people might like to learn for the sake of learning, that isn't a strong motivation. However, knowing that your family will be taken care of after you die, that's a powerful driver.

What do your customers want to know before working

with you, and after working with you? Remember, that "knowing" something is a form of security and if you approach the events which happen in your customers day, from the perspective of "what would they like to know now?" you'll find out what they want confidence with.

For example, I want to know that I'm heading in the right direction with my business. I want to know I'm doing the best for my child. When I open my emails, I want to know that it'll be full of leads. When I have a complaint come in, I want to know that my team will handle it and take it off my plate.

"Knowing" is a collective term for:

1. Confidence
2. Clarity
3. Certainty
4. Assuredness
5. Predictability
6. Insight

When someone says they want to know something, they're looking for answers that tell them yes or no. Apart from feelings, I believe that knowledge is the number one thing that people are looking for. They want to know they're on the right path or at least the best path for them. We all live in an uncertain frame of mind and the more we "know" the more confidence we have.

"Now, after working with you, I know how much I'll make

each month. I know that my staff will get paid and I know the plan for the business to take us to the next level."

That's a powerful statement for a customer to make and one that you should be leaning into.

Meet

Moving more into status, meeting people is all about your network. So who do your customers want to meet? Who do they want to network with and spend time with? Who do they meet now, who they'd rather not see again. Who do they meet now, who they'd want to spend more time with?

Meeting people that you look up to could be professional or personal. Perhaps you help business owners take more time off so they can meet their favourite athletes. Or maybe you help them speak on stage with someone they admire.

Depending on who your customer is, they may or may not have a strong desire to meet certain people. If they do, this is an extremely powerful benefit and motivator. The desire to increase the value of our network, speaks to our desire to increase our own worth. If your customer wants to be popular, well-loved and a high status, there will almost certainly be people that they want to meet and network with.

On the other hand, meeting people could be more of an objective based desire. For example the desire to meet a personal trainer and work with them every day. The desire to meet a partner and find love. Maybe they want to meet the right business partner or general manager to start growing their business. Maybe they just want to meet more customers themselves.

Status

We're into the final two big benefits and motivators here. Status and moral struggle.

Starting with status, status is all about who we are and what we want to become. Status is a perception of yourself and how you see yourself. Or, in many cases, how you think other people see you. It's also a question of how you want other people to see you.

Before working with you, your customers are seen as[blank] by themselves/by their partner/by their friends etc.

After working with you, your customers are seen as[blank] by other people/by their competition/by their colleagues.

People either want to become their role model (albeit with a twist) or they want to be seen as a title. For example "I want to be the Elon Musk of accounting". Hell, some people might just say they want to be Elon Musk. That's a role model status.

Others might say "I want to be the most dangerous player in the bookkeeping industry" whatever that means. That's more of a title.

Status is a powerful motivator and benefit because it demonstrates transformation. To go from "layabout, lazy, overweight midnight-snacker" to "disciplined, fit and healthy go-getter" is a visual, easy to understand and demonstrable transformation. From "stressed and overworked Mum" to "Mum of the year" is a clear progression.

Every day, people work towards who they think they are. At least, who they think they deserve to be. The world's most prolific book writer is a status and could even be measurable. It's unlikely that one person would ever claim that title, but anyone who does have that status desire will continue working towards it.

Interestingly, some people's desired status is to remain exactly where they are. They don't value themselves or respect themselves enough to want better. That is of course their prerogative and it might seem sad to you (and in many cases it is), but it's of VITAL importance that you don't waste energy trying to change that.

Status is a deeply internal process. What we think of ourselves and our own self-image is completely under the control of ourself. You can't convince someone to be something they don't want to. At least not for long. And if you can, the motivation isn't there long enough for it to be sustainable.

Think about parents who push their children to become doctors or engineers or any other profession. The reality is that if the person doesn't want to be that "thing" or have that status or title, they'll be unhappy, unmotivated and burn out.

We're constantly strengthening and reaffirming our current self-image. Our status is something we either protect, or work on. But that works with people who want to change and be a better version of themselves, as much as it works with people who don't want to change.

Take our layabout, lazy, overweight midnight-snacker from earlier. Let's say that we have two people who fit this bill and one of them (claiming to be happy with it) feels that they don't deserve to be better or do anything different. Another one does want to make the change and feels they're allowed to be better.

The one who wants to stay the same, will do everything they can to reinforce their identity as who they are now. Everything from arguing about facts and evidence, to seeing only problems and reasons they can't change. The one who wants to change will be more open to change, look for opportunities to move towards their different status and find more people who support their viewpoint.

If you can discover or talk about the desired status that people do want to become, you've got a powerful benefit and transformation. Arguably, the most powerful motivation. But don't assume that everyone in your niche wants to become that status or title. Not everyone wants to be Mum of the year, or the world's most dangerous accountant. So find a status that you want people to become and encourage that.

Moral struggle

This is the hardest to understand, but an absolute gamechanger if you can fully get to grips with it. All humans have an internal moral struggle that they're battling every day. Of course, many of us deal with multiple moral choices every day. And we all have a deeper driving purpose which we're working towards.

The interesting thing about "morals" is that they're totally and utterly subjective. You might even say that they're made up and fictional. What was moral in Mesopotamia 5000 BC would be very different to what was considered moral in 12th Century England. Even by modern standards the concepts of moral right and wrong has shifted massively in the last 100 years, or even 50 years. To this end, it's pretty safe to say, we all feel pretty strongly about some stuff, and not others.

Your product, when all is said and done, is contributing to and strengthening a moral conviction that your customer has. Maybe even a few. This might seem WAY deeper than a standard sales book, but one of my moral convictions is that sales needs to dive deep into the lives of our customers and make their life better. Businesses who really really REALLY care about their customers, stand out. Businesses that treat customers like a number or a sale or a dollar symbol, are weak.

Sell Futures, Not Features

Here's some questions to ask yourself about your customers:

1. What do my customers believe they're entitled to or they have a right to?

2. What do my customers feel they deserve?

3. What are my customer's values? What do they focus on?

4. If my customers gave advice about living the best life possible, what would that advice be?

5. What do your customers believe they should be doing with their life?

The best and easiest example of "moral struggle" for a customer set, is new parents. Many new parents believe that the absolute prime thing they need to do now, for their new child, is do everything they can to look after them. You might read that and think "duh". But let's really take a look at that struggle.

I must do the best thing for my child.

First, there are plenty of parents who do not care about their kids. They don't want to do best for them, they're not even interested in wanting the best for their child. No matter how wealthy, educated, privileged, poor, hard-working or experienced a person is, the priority of giving your child the best in life is not a guarantee just because you have a child.

Secondly "the best" means a lot of different things to

different people. The best for your child might mean a happy healthy life, it might mean an eternity in paradise after death, it might mean giving them everything they want, it might mean being unemotional and distant with them.

£1000 baby stroller? Absolutely you must have that if you care about your child at all. $1000's of toys at Christmas? Of course! Loads of books and sleep and a good diet? Obviously that's the best you can give. All purchasing decisions are emotional. The moral struggle that your customers are facing is the driving force behind those emotions and therefor, those decisions. People have very deep beliefs and they'll do anything they can to realise those beliefs.

The rise of eco-friendly and low-carbon products and services proves that people are willing to change their buying behaviour to do what they feel is right for the planet. Does that mean that an eco-friendly product will outsell a normal or more established product? Not necessarily. Because while environmentally friendly products might be high on someone's values, convenience or quality or price or "I just need to get to work and earn some money" might be higher.

It might also not match their morals in the right way. In the example above I gave 3 examples on how to do best by your child. Each one would be considered an obvious choice for different people. Some people would value the stroller over books, or Christmas over a stroller. The moral struggle that your business is helping with, might be the right moral aim, but the wrong method.

It's also important to remember that humans are really good at compartmentalising. This means allowing one moral to be strong within certain circumstances, and another moral to take over in other circumstances. As paradoxical as it sounds, it's incredibly common and we're all guilty of it. The same people who buy environmentally friendly dish soap or cleaning products don't bat an eyelid at buying a new car or fridge. The same person who demands the best for their child won't hesitate to buy products from a company that uses child labour.

What this means, is that the moral stance you put behind your product might not make any impact at all, unless the customer matches the type of moral, the method of that moral and the circumstances of that moral. When I worked in data security at a large corporation, the company and board and CEO and all the staff constantly banged on about being more environmentally conscious. It was all the rage and we did all kinds of "green initiative" stuff.

We were being pitched for a new server farm that massively affected our carbon footprint. The specs were roughly the same as the current setup, but the heat from the servers (server farms get extremely hot) was used to heat the water in the building. The cost was more expensive, of course, and required an initial upfront investment. It would have suited our environmentally conscious façade beautifully, but they didn't go for it. Why? Money of course. Specifically, shareholder money. The company felt they had a moral imperative to serve the shareholder first, above all else. Therefor the ultimate moral sale went to the business who could secure the best profit margin.

The point to that story is that you absolutely must understand the moral struggles that your customers face. Some will be obvious and some will be hidden. But if you can build benefits that demonstrate a better relationship, or happier childhood, or more respect from your shareholders, people will buy. But they'll only buy based on their deeper moral beliefs. People are very good at talking about their morals, but the best way to really see them is with where they place their wallet.

If you're completely overwhelmed or confused by this last section, don't worry. I was too. But I found later that I was overcomplicating it. I was making it harder than it needed to be. During a quiet moment, I asked, "what do my customers really care about? What actually matters to them?"

Family, security, being able to provide, being a stable role model. It's the ability to be self-reliant and to provide for their family. Before working with me, customers struggle to always provide for their family, after working with me they can easier provide for their family more than they first thought they could.

What's weird about that, is that it's also my moral driving force. By extension, all the work and effort I exert is to do the same thing. When it all boils down, I'm just trying to do the best for my family. By extension that's what most of my customers and readers like you, are also trying to do.

Writing benefits

In the next chapter, we'll talk about writing up all these notes and pieces into definable benefits. But frankly you're not that far off now. If you have 5 solid sentences that you can write out, that follow "before working with me…after working with me…" then you've got some killer benefits ready to go.

What we're trying to do is move away from listing a load of stuff that your product or service is, and start to redefine your product by the things it does. Why is life better in the future after working with you? After buying that motorbike how do people feel? When they eat at your restaurant what are they feeling? When someone finishes a coaching session from you, why do they feel good about themselves?

Almost every aspect of your sales pitch, marketing, messaging, blog content, podcasts and website needs to focus on those futures and benefits. Those feelings are what you need to amplify and promote, because they're what people are really looking for. Grab a piece of paper or your notebook and start to write these all out. There will be a pattern and lots of overlap. There will be a running theme through your benefits and futures, distilling down what it is that you really do. With your new list of benefits, have a think about why all that matters. Why are you helping people achieve and get those kinds of futures? Why would you want to help someone reach those futures? Why do you do what you do? It's a big question for sure. There are entire books based to just that question and after working on my own "why" for a long time, I found the simplest and easiest method for discovering a core driving motivation, is to talk to myself.

I took my list of benefits and futures and I went into a quiet room with myself and my phone. I used the recording app to talk to myself for around 45 minutes, asking "why does this stuff matter to me?" I just let myself talk. It was awkward and clumsy. I felt very stupid and I made a lot of false starts. There were pauses and silences for what felt like minutes. But eventually, after I settled past the feeling of narcissism, I started talking to myself. I was telling stories, revealing memories that I never wanted to repeat, memories of events that I didn't want others to go through.

Within 45 minutes I had discovered a very deeper and core purpose to why I sold the things I sold. I connected with it on a greater level. If you're thinking that you sell laptops or animal bedding or white paint, and that you have no chance of connecting to a deeper why, you're not thinking deep enough.

There is pride to finding depth in what you sell, no matter what you sell. Do you know the #1 thing that people are looking for, above all else? The #1 benefit that every business should sell, many businesses promise but seldom few deliver on? The #1 benefit that all customers are looking for is a reliable supplier. That's it. A reliable supplier who lives up to their expectations. A reliable supplier that delivers on a promise.

Yes you might just sell white paint. But what about the buying process? What about using the paint and how does it hold up over time? Will you gladly help and refund someone who's had a bad batch? If I buy your white paint, will I regret it? Or will it just work and I don't have to complain or get an exchange? There is a lot to be said for being proud of doing what you're doing and doing it well.

Typical dull statement - I am a designer

Many web designers, graphic designers and marketers vastly play down what it is that they do. I call it "the designer's paradox" because a designer will refer to themselves as "just a designer" in order to not show off or stick their neck out. But in the same breath they'll gladly critique another's design work and say it's terrible. Then, they'll switch again after seeing some different design work and say "that's so good I could never do that."

Perhaps upon reflection we all do that to some extent. We all think everyone else's job is easy, that ours is difficult and that we're the only ones who can do our work just how we like it, but then there are also loads of other people better than us who we are afraid to compete against.

When someone asks "what do you do?" they're not asking for a job title. Partly because it's just a polite question that people ask at parties, the gym, sacrificial orgies, that kind of thing. Partly because most people don't know what most jobs are. You've got the big players like doctors, police, fireman, teacher, writer. But even then, most people don't know what you do during that job.

Telling someone you're an operations efficiencies coordinator could mean that you're a logistics manager working on $30 million projects. Or you put stock back on the shelves in grocery shops. What people want is a micro story that tells them the type of adventures you go on.

Job titles like designer and coordinator and operations technician were invented by managers and human resource directors so they could understand their own business. It's like labelling your snack cupboard or how my Mum organises her tea (lots of different types, tastes, occasions and times for different teas). A job title tells you where you fit within a wider organisation and is useful to two people. The HR

127

director, and your manager.

When you're telling anyone else what you do, don't tell them what your manager calls you. Don't tell them something you understand. Tell them something they understand. Put it into context that gives them an idea of the type of work you do, the results you get and the BENEFITS you bring. Tell them the types of futures that you create.

Killer statement - I turn email addresses into monthly paying customers

A designer could work on websites, marketing, graphics, print, branding, fonts and so many more things. If you want to start uncovering what your products and services do, and make more sales, you need to uncover what you do and what you bring to the table.

Take a web designer for example. Let's say that they have a ton of skills and through the exercise above they realise that their strong point is creating landing pages on websites. They like to work with subscription-based businesses and their sweet spot is landing pages that collect email addresses and sales pages that sell products.

Rather than call themselves a designer, they've answered with question "what do you do?" by finishing the sentence "after working with me, my customers..." and in this case, their customers find monthly subscription customers from email addresses. If this is absolute nonsense and gobbledegook to you, don't worry about the immediate example. Just think about the core, best result that you deliver to customers. What do they get in the future?

A trap that many people fall into is making their job sound more complex than it is/needs to be. "I'm a conversion optimisation specialist technician". Very very impressive no doubt and someone who calls themselves a CEO or director of a 2-person company is also clearly, a big swinging dick. However the only person you're impressing is yourself. If I can't understand it, I don't care about it. Keep bringing it back to "what does someone get after working with me?" In the future, after working with me, people can… and then use the prompts we've talked about above. You don't need to make a sale or lead in the first 10 seconds of meeting someone. Just tell them the result you get and they'll understand. If they're NOT interested, great! That means they'll be a good referrer or colleague. If they do get it and want to learn more – they could well be a lead.

You can get a copy of our Killer Statement worksheet, plus 8 other exercises at

sellfuturesnotfeatures.com/workbook.

We'll send you the worksheets that accompany this book for free, straight to your email. Studies show that action takers DO the work and write things down – that's what makes them real.

Summary:

- Products and services become more interesting when they tell a story about the person buying them

- Lean into the fluffy, illogical and emotional side of what you're selling

- You could change someone's entire day going forward from the moment they buy. If you're looking to increase sales, first look at how it affects the customer's life

- You're not defined by what you do, but by the change you bring into the lives of your customers. Stop defining yourself by what you sell and start defining yourself by who you help and how they are helped

Chapter 4 - Sell futures

Structuring the offer to become compelling

Sell futures not features

You'll be sick of this phrase by the time you finish this book. Sell futures not features is a way of restructuring your entire pitch and sales method. It's the lens through which successful sales are made and can completely flip a customer's perception about you and the product. More than that, it's a fantastic re-framing device to solve problems. If a product isn't selling, ask yourself "what's the future we're selling here?" If the future isn't obvious, it's a good point to start exploring.

We're sold futures from a very early age. What do you want to be when you grow up? Work hard and you'll get a good job. We're also sold futures while we work. Pensions, retirement, holidays, Christmas breaks. The difference of course comes when you realise you might want a different future to someone else.

In this chapter we're going to talk about the act of selling the benefits that you've just come up with in the previous chapter. In chapter 2 we created a series of benefits that are desirable and compelling. In this chapter we're going to further convert them into saleable futures and structure them in a way that is easier to say and market.

For example one of the benefits we uncovered in the last chapter was "find monthly subscription customers from email addresses". We can re-word that statement and the other "before/after" statements into clear messages that are easier to say, pitch and write.

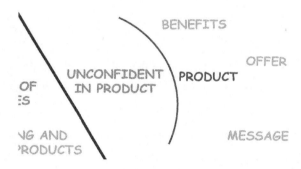

Figure 10: Products are Benefits, Offers and a Message

Benefit bucket/sales ammunition

One of my secret weapons is a bucket of benefits for all the products that I sell. It's like sales ammunition that I can pull out and use whenever I create marketing copy or sales copy. Everything from sales emails, to pages, to webinars and YouTube videos can use the benefits in my bucket and make my life easier.

It might sound bizarre having a list of benefits for a product, but too often I see businesses focus on one thing that

132

their product does, rather than showing everything it does. Deep down at its core your product probably does one thing, but the benefits it provides are varied and many. A car has loads of benefits, an iPad has lots of benefits, a tax accountant has lots of benefits.

Not all the benefits will be useful for all situations. But it's important to list as many as you can and have them to hand. Some benefits will suit certain people and certain types of customers or personalities. Other times they'll suit certain messages or campaigns that you're running. It's also a process of discovery for yourself, understanding why people would buy from you. It might sound obvious but I see businesses who can't give me more than 2 or 3 reasons to buy all the time. It's a pretty simple idea, if you can't think of more reasons why someone should buy your product, compared to why they feel they shouldn't, you're going to struggle making sales.

We've got the Benefit Bullet worksheet available for FREE at sellfuturesnotfeatures.com/workbook.

You'll also get the rest of the worksheets, sent straight to your emails for free (plus there's some extra bonus training that we only share with readers of this book).

Killer bullet points

When I used to do door to door sales I worked with a guy called Charlie. Charlie was a very well spoken, tall, handsome guy who would constantly do hilarious things. One of his classic "pranks" was to buy a brand new £45,000 BMW and park it down the road from his parents, hop back in his old car and drive that car home so they wouldn't know he'd just spent a ton of money on a new car. Classic Charlie.

Charlie also had an incredible talent for selling TV packages door to door. Basically what we did was sell satellite TV subscriptions all over the South West of England. It was hard work, uncomfortable and the pay wasn't great. However, the people were fun, we were young lads looking to make some money and we'd usually get a beer bought for us at the end of the day. Charlie's sales technique was unlike anything I'd ever seen before. He would sell pretty costly satellite TV packages without one mention of what the product was.

The hardest part of door to door is getting in the door. Once you're inside people let their guards down and you can open the conversation up. Of course everyone says that they'd never let a door to door salesperson in their house, but it's a numbers game. And Charlie had a special tactic for selling. What Charlie would do is make the opening pitch all about the customer. Even if he knew literally nothing about them, he'd focus the sales pitch on them rather than the TV subscription and he'd speak almost entirely in bullet points.

Knock on the door

Customer: hello?

Sell Futures, Not Features

Charlie:

- ☐ Hi there! Did you know that your TV won't work in a few months?

- ☐ That's right, old TVs need to be upgraded to digital signals

- ☐ Luckily you don't have to buy a new TV

- ☐ We're offering a digital signal upgrade courtesy of Sky

- ☐ Are you happy losing your TV signal?

- ☐ How would you feel if you couldn't watch TV anymore?

- ☐ Would you like me to show you how to keep your TV signal going?

Reading through that script looks more like a landing page than a door-to-door conversation. Charlie understood that as soon as someone opens the door, their guard is up and they don't want to buy anything. Most of the guys selling d2d would try to "sell" straight away. They would ask questions and introduce themselves. In sales theory, you're taught all of this, but Charlie knew that he first had to get them to pay attention. Every second you spend introducing yourself, v "how do I tell them to go away?"

Read through those bullet points again. Every single one of them is essentially a headline. Each one could be a subject line of an email, or a YouTube video title. They're all designed to get a response from a customer and have them listen to you and pay attention.

Not every sales interaction needs to be like this, structured in this way. But let's look at the typical sales journey. Knocking on someone's door is the equivalent of an advert. It's interrupting their normal routine and disrupting them. Just like an advert, Charlie knew he had to talk like a clickbait article or headline in order to get them to pay attention. It might sound weird and read weird but to the customer he's just getting to the point.

Every bullet point is also a benefit. They might not read like typical standard benefits, but they are. A benefit is just a better future version of something (or someone). It stirs emotion and in some cases, threatens to take something away from people. In the 1970s Amos Tversky and Daniel Kahneman researched the principle of "Loss Aversion". A psychological phenomenon that people would rather work to protect a loss, than to gain something more[1].

Charlie understood this perfectly and knew that taking away the TV was a more powerful attention grabber, than to offer more TV. What we were trying to sell is a satellite TV subscription, but Charlie knew that we couldn't get to the sales part until we'd crossed the attention part. They had to want to learn more, and the easiest way to do that, was

---

[1] https://en.wikipedia.org/wiki/Loss_aversion

frontloading the conversation like an advert and getting their attention, mainly through telling them what they'd lose out on.

In this next section, we're going to create a series of benefits as bullet points and use them as ammunition for all your sales copy. Your messaging, promotions, adverts, pitches, videos, blog posts, landing pages, subject lines – we're going to create a lot of them. These bullet points have been gathered from years of copy research and thousands of sales pages, pitches, blog posts, adverts and headlines. If you want to get really really good at writing these, try to write out 5 per template. It's a great exercise.

How to [benefit]

- How to finally shift that weight you've picked up and get in better shape than you were, 10 years ago
- How to find the top paying customers within your market and make YOU the obvious choice to buy
- How to generate more sales per day (without adding strain on your operations and delivery)

[Action verb] - [benefit]

- Explode the number of people within your network that want to refer you to their friends
- Discover the hidden secret to losing weight that Gladiators, Spartans and Batman all know
- Finally pay for advertising and new leads and know exactly what works

137

Sell Futures, Not Features

 # ways to [benefit]

1. 3 ways to earn money while you sleep and 1 mistake that all marketers make

2. 5 ignored and hidden supermarket herbs that Michelin Star chefs know (and are dead cheap)

3. 3 stages to make sales on automation without spending more on advertising

Better than [action/alternative] - [benefit]

1. Better than buying new marketing funnel software. Customers DO NOT CARE what kind of marketing funnel software you use and this costs 1/12 of what new marketing funnel software costs

2. Better than social media marketing. Start generating leads and referrals TODAY, not in weeks or months' time using social media groups to slowly build a following

3. Better than selling graphic design, SEO or web design. See how we attract customers and leads without even explaining WHAT we do and why the customer is grateful that you don't tell them that stuff

Do you [headache] Are you [headache]?

1. Do you suffer from writer's block? Never sure what to write for your blog content? From ideas to topics, titles and entire posts - follow our process to write killer blog content faster and easier than ever

2. Do you suffer from bloating after starting your new diet? Are you tired of feeling full AND hungry at the same time?

3. Ever had another driver blind you when driving at night? Sick of having bright lights shine into your eyes making it dangerous to drive when its dark?

It's not your fault that you [action]

- It's not your fault that you've invested in Facebook ads and it hasn't worked out
- If you've ever tried losing weight and couldn't keep it off, it's NOT your fault (here's why)
- Can you remember the last time you cooked a simple meal and it all went wrong? There's a basic reason why and it's not your fault

[Action word] – [benefit]

- Finally! No more distractions at work!
- Explode the number of LinkedIn requests you get, asking to connect
- Uncover the hidden secret to Facebook ads and drive dirt cheap traffic

The truth behind/about [action/benefit]

- The truth behind exercise equipment and why it doesn't help you lose weight
- The key to making sales is a 3 part follow up system – which we call 1e 2e 3e.

⬜ Discover the hidden truth to quitting smoking, drinking and gambling that causes most people to quit in the first 2 weeks

Better than [alternative]

- Better than cold calling! If you're looking for new leads, get them cheaper and faster with this
- This blows "online courses" out of the water. Why drag and drop apps are the future of scaling
- More powerful than SEO. Start getting traffic to your website in hours not months

You might be reading these and thinking that a lot of them just read like headlines. Worse still, a lot of them read like "click bait" headlines. The cold hard truth is that these types of headlines and bullet points WORK. They grab attention, focus on the reader and deliver a story.

If you decided to use a series of bullet points like this and fail to deliver on the promise of the copy, then yes, that would be click bait. If I see a YouTube tutorial that says "Finally! Learn how to advertise on Instagram for FREE (without wasting a penny)" and it failed to deliver on that promise, then that title was absolutely click bait.

However I'm not asking you to deliver click bait, I'm asking you to punch up your benefits so that they're easy to read. If you think that your product or service is "above" direct response style copy like this, you're wrong. Absolutely

140

every single business on the planet could benefit from tightening up their benefits and making them more interesting to read.

These are essentially, headlines. They're designed to catch the fleeting and fickle attention of your audience and get them to stick around. People might turn their noses up at copy like this, but that's usually because they're either a) afraid of what other people might think or b) afraid of trying something new. Advertising, blog posts, videos, podcasts, social posts, sales letters, pitches, presentations, websites, slogans. The list of applications for content like this is endless AND they become more effective the more you use them.

Direct response micro-copy like this is easier for people to read and understand. It's faster to grasp and gets attention. If you feel that your customers spend more time listening to your competitors and buying their products, then this is how you level the playing field.

You could write an entire pitch, cold open, sales letter or advert using one or all of these bullet points. There are literally hundreds more examples available all over the internet. It's a sad fact that incredible products and smart people don't get the recognition that they deserve. History is overflowing with those talented individuals who are technically the best in their field. So why don't they reap the rewards of their success? Because the world's best photographer will make fewer sales than the world's best salesperson.

Bestselling books aren't "best written" or "best read." They are best sellers because they sell better than other books. If photographers, accountants, developers, movies, podcasts, YouTube channels, apps, composers, singers, chefs and co-working spaces spent just 5% of their time working on marketing themselves and writing out this kind of copy, they'd see results faster than they expect.

Not all the bullet points will work. Some will fall flat and be ignored. Great! Then you're slowly learning what your audience responds to and what they want more of. Which leads me onto our final point for this chapter.

Sell before you build

"Mike, what's the best way for me to create and sell a course?" During 2020 this was the most common question I was asked. Despite spending years telling people to create scalable products, it was only when face to face contact was made difficult, did people want to take the plunge.

Frankly, this question could be the same for absolutely any product or service.

- How do you set up a blog?
- How do you start making money with YouTube?
- How can I write and sell a book?

From apps to courses to software and events, everyone has

the next idea that they think will take them and their business to the next level. And what happens when they launch their new product or venture?

Nothing. Absolutely nothing happens.

I see this so much that it breaks my heart. People pour time, money, energy and resources into creating a product which they think the market is dying for. You see it on Shark Tank, Dragons Den, KickStarter, IndieGoGo, Facebook and other networking places. Someone has created something and they think it'll change the world. The only problem is that no one else thinks so.

They struggle to make any sales and they're confused and upset as to why it hasn't sold. They followed the process, took all the right steps. That online course on launching products that they took, told them all about setting up a website and how to make sales online. They did everything right, so why isn't it selling?

Because they haven't sold it – they've just built it.

Getting so stuck inside your own head, is cancer to product launches. I've seen it working inside large corporations, mid-sized businesses, small and micro-businesses. The business owner or manager or director, thinks that "the world needs X, therefor we should build it!"

They think that their current customers buy stuff from them, so it makes sense that they'll buy this too. Or if the business is starting from scratch, they have a mentality of "build it and they will come". Like building a massive glass covered hyper modern 72 story, £500 million building, only to have most of the space inside it totally empty. Because no one wants it. That's the London Shard I'm referring to. And it's not alone.

There are spaces like this around the world that have suffered the same fate. Ultra-expensive inflated monuments to short-sighted egocentricity, that will never ever fulfil the "ground-breaking vision" of the designer. And the same goes for courses, apps, software, business ideas, products, services and entire industries. If you invest all your time building the "thing", when it comes to launch day you need to spend 2X time and money on selling it.

When movies launch, they'll roughly spend 1x – 2x the production budget on marketing, trailers and advertising. Which means that if a film costs $100 million, they'll spend another $100 million (minimum) on getting people's attention. Even for massive film franchises like the Marvel Cinematic Universe, the studio will spend millions on advertising to get the word out and tell people why they can go and see it. Which means that a film needs to make DOUBLE its budget to start to turn a profit. The vast majority of movies do not make a profit[2]. It's a high-risk venture

---

2

because you're putting all your hopes on selling tickets AFTER the product is released.

In your business, you have the massive advantage of selling a product before it's even released. We can do this on a micro-level, testing what the world wants to see. And then at a larger scale selling five, six and seven figure products and services before they're developed.

If you're planning a brand-new product, or even a new campaign for a product, you need to think "sell first, build second". Sell before we build. Lots of businesses are afraid of this however, because again, ABS (anything but sales). They're afraid that if they go to market and try to sell a product, and no one buys, then they'll look stupid. First of all, you won't. Second of all even if you did look stupid, you'd look a lot more stupid if you didn't make any sales after building a product.

"But what if only a few people sign up or buy?" Some products have a break-even threshold, which is understandable. Other products might need a minimum number of sales or customers to work. No problem. You'll have to work out what a successful "launch" looks like in terms of units sold, revenue and profit. Compared to time to build, costs and resources, you'll absolutely have to work out

https://www.forbes.com/sites/schuylermoore/2019/01/03/most-films-lose-money/?sh=25cfd085739f what a successful launch looks like. And if you make ZERO sales? No big deal, close the cart and move on to try something else. If you do make some sales but not quite enough, you have a couple of options.

Either refund the sales and try again. Or, can you restructure the product and offer to deliver the results/benefits but profitably? Ask the buyers and let them know the situation. Offer refunds, change the offer and move on. Be open and people will work with you. If you don't make the sales you want, you've just saved yourself a ton of time and money. Because the market has told you one of three things.

- You don't have a big enough audience to launch this product to yet
- Your messaging/hooks/benefits aren't clear or compelling enough
- Your customers don't want that

It's not all three that cause failures, though it can be a combination. The reason I love this kind of feedback is that we can scale down the initial tests and launch larger products and services down the line.

10 step launch process

- Here's how to run a product launch campaign from scratch.
- Reach out to your audience and ask them "what are you struggling with?"

- Email, social, message etc.
- Get them to tell you what THEY want more of
- Create 5 bullet points with benefits related to those replies
- Create content for all 5 bullets (using the bullet as a headline)
- See what gets the most traffic, engagement etc.
- Take the most popular content and create some gated training/content around it
- Do people optin/sign up? Do people care about this enough to give personal information?
- Invite people to some sales content (webinar, training, event, sales letter) and sell a solution to that problem.
- Do people buy?

Reach out to your audience and ask them "what are you struggling with?"

As I've mentioned earlier, many businesses assume that whatever they produce is a good idea and people will want to buy. Unfortunately you couldn't be further from the truth.

The absolute first step to launching a new product is to first ask your audience "what are you struggling with?" Customers, leads, your network, audience, followers. You need to ask them what they are struggling with, not assuming that you know.

If you don't have an audience, go and get one. Research on forums, ask to join groups, or pay to get answers. I cannot stress this enough.

YOU ABSOLUTELY CATEGORICALLY NEED AN AUDIENCE TO LAUNCH A PRODUCT SUCCESSFULY

I see time and time again, smart, passionate and well-meaning business owners create and launch a product to zero fanfare and worse, zero sales. I know this is hard work and building an audience is a long process. You can absolutely speed up the process and buy audience with paid ads and social content. But that requires a budget. Either spend time to build an audience organically or make sure that you have a few thousand dollars to test, launch and promote a product.

Does that add time onto your projection? Probably. Do you need to make sales and money now? Almost certainly. But let's look at the two options.

- ⬜ Spend time and/or money building an audience to whom you can successfully launch products to and grow over time, making more certain sales when you do eventually launch

- ⬜ Spend time and budget building a product that no one buys or even knows about, and trying to do that over and over?

If you think you need to make money now, I've got bad

news for you. Even with a successful product launch, it's not going to make you millions overnight. It's a long process and takes time. And if you think you're desperate for sales and leads now, I can assure you that you'll be even more desperate when your next product fails to launch again.

If you take anything from this chapter, please let it be that you need to reach out to your audience of prospects, customers, leads, followers, networks and groups and ask them what they want help with. Get them to tell you what they'll buy.

How to know what people will buy

- There's a few ways you can ask this question:
- What's stressing you out right now?
- What do you wish you had more of?
- What do you wish you had less of?
- What could be better in your life right now?
- What's your goal for the next 90 days?
- What's your goal for the next 30 days?
- What's your goal for the next year?
- What needs fixing in your life?
- If I could wave a magic wand and fix something right now, what would it be?

People will gladly tell you what they're looking to buy and what they want fixed. You might believe that their real problem is cashflow management or eating too much. But the reality is that if they don't believe that's the problem, you can't sell a solution to itYou need to get the language that your audience are using.

It's the difference between what I want and what I need. You can only sell things that people want. If they want and need it, great. But if they don't want it, but they do need it, they'll choose the thing they want almost every time.

The world needs to adopt a more plant-based diet. All evidence points to people needing to cut down the amount of meat they consume. But what do people want? People want burgers and bacon and chicken.

You need to get the language that your audience is using, and you need to see what they're thinking about. Don't guess this. Don't assume or think you already know. You don't. And what comes back will be enlightening.

What if your audience responds with a problem that you're already trying to solve? Then continue promoting your current products or create a new one. One with a higher price and a higher profit margin.

If you get "sick" of solving the same problems over and over, you're in the wrong game. I know that for my audience, niche, leads and client are their #1 concerns. Do I believe that their real problems are scale, mindset and confidence? Of course. But I'm here to solve their problems. If it happens that I sell a solution designed to get them sales and leads, but the solution is addressing confidence and mindset, I'm delivering what they need and selling them what they want.

Vegan and vegetarian companies are beginning to see this too. They don't sell the idea that people should eat more vegetables and less meat. They're selling weight loss, cheaper food bills, better taste, faster cooking times, less washing up etc. They're selling futures, not features.

By the way, you can get our entire overview 9 step roadmap to help you sell futures not features by heading to sellfuturesnotfeatures.com/workbook.

We'll send you the worksheets that accompany this book for free, straight to your email. Plus, you can follow the exercises along in this book and be one of the action takers.

Summary:

- ▪ Benefits are how someone's life is better after you work with them. They're hard to replace and they remove problems, reach goals or both

- ▪ Benefit bullet points can be blog post titles, product headlines, taglines and slogans. They're bullet points in sales copy, paragraph headings, campaign hooks and more

- ▪ The ability to sum up a product or service into a punchy desirable compelling benefit that's easy to understand and clearly directed at a specific user is the single biggest advantage that you can bring to your marketing and sales communication

☐ Push and pull between pain and reward, problems and goals. The tension between light and dark in one benefit or between two benefits is what builds excitement, anticipation and desire

Chapter 5 - Qualification

Making sure that you're talking to the right customer

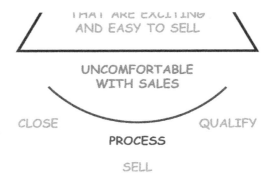

THAT ARE EXCITING
AND EASY TO SELL

UNCOMFORTABLE
WITH SALES

CLOSE   QUALIFY

PROCESS

SELL

Figure 11: A great sales process is just Qualifying, Selling and Closing

Qualification call

Qualifying the customer is about making sure of 5 key points.

1. They can afford to work with you

2. They can afford to put your advice into practice

3. You can help them get incredible results

4. You want to work with them/like them

5. They refer

As business owners and salespeople, we're often told "be thankful for what you're getting. Beggars can't be choosers." If you've ever sent a proposal to a lead and had them respond by sucking air through their teeth, whistling and saying "we don't have that kind of money", you know how important qualification is.

Qualification is more than just making sure they can afford you though. It's also making sure that they can afford your advice. If a customer buys your products and services, only to learn that they need to build X as well, in order to get results, can make you seem like the bad guy. It's like selling someone a car only for them to become outraged that they are the ones who have to buy the fuel too.

When we work with customers, we want to make sure that they get the best results possible. This isn't always easy but it's made easier by only working with people who you can actually help. Qualification is about making sure that they'll benefit from working with you. This might sound odd to say, but as we've explored above, we can help anyone – we just can't help everyone.

There are customers who just aren't going to see any benefits from working with you. Or at least won't see as many benefits compared to other people. Imagine working with a sports coach who helps you breathe better and last longer underwater when swimming. For most people, the exercises would be useful, but chances are unless you swim underwater a lot, like as an underwater hockey player, you're not going to benefit as much as someone who does swim underwater a lot.

Specifically, it's about asking yourself if you can add

massive value to them and their life.

Finally, do you even want to work with this person? I remember being approached by an investment banker who was looking to branch out on his own and start selling courses and a few other digital products. He had an audience, relative authority and a pretty decent idea. The problem was that he was an unbearable cretin. I realised that I probably wouldn't work with him when he referred to his wife as a "7/10". Wanker.

But it's not just about the people (although that can swing a vote). Do you care about their business or their problems? Do you really care about the situation they're in? Large corporate businesses just don't interest me. Although a mad and charming CEO can often sway my mind.

The Call, is the part of the process where we're discovering if we're right for each other. Earlier, I defined sales as "working out if it makes sense for two parties to work together". Qualification is the first barrier.

Don't overcomplicate the call and setting up a meeting. Unless you've already spoken to the person before, it's best to keep a qualification call as the main call to action that you're trying to get people to take. For example, if you run adverts that have people land on your website, asking them to enter their email address for a free report or tool, the next most immediate thing would be to try and get them on a call or a meeting.

If you think of the qualification process as a checklist, the 5 items above make a good starting point. The mistake many people make is trying to sell or close on the first call. Or worse still, trying to get someone who they've never met on a "free 15 minute call". I've never understood these messages and emails, I get them a lot from LinkedIn. "Hey MICHAEL KILLEN – FOUNDER OF SELL YOUR SERVICE LIMITED. I love your product and/or service and I know that my performance marketing agency can add a massive amount of value to your business. Do you have time for a quick free 15-minute call?"

These kinds of cold messages scream desperation and laziness. You know full well that you've received messages like this. If you're unsure as to why you don't like them, let me explain. And, if you've committed this sin of cold outreach before, let's explore how to make it better. First, offering a "free call" from the side of the seller is like offering a "leak free bottle". As the buyer, I fully expect the call to be free, just as I expect the bottle to hold water with no leaks. That isn't unique or a benefit. The rule of thumb with statements like that is "would my competitor say the opposite?" I.e., would someone else send a cold message to a lead and say "Hey Mike, I'd love to get on a call at your cost for 15 minutes"? Of course not. Therefor you shouldn't say it.

If someone wouldn't say the opposite, you don't have to say the obvious.

The second area it fails at is specificity. The #1 golden rule of qualification is "am I talking to the right person?" This is the #1 thing you need to think about before sending any kind of message or outreach. Even at a networking event, webinar, training course or online content, the question you should be asking before you even get on a call with the customer is "does this person have the potential to be a customer?"

Let's say that you send 100 outreach messages to 100 different business owners on LinkedIn. If the message is well crafted and specific, it'll read something like the below.

"Hey Sarah, we haven't met but I've had the fortune of coming across your profile. I understand that you're the marketing manager for AMTar. I've got a free tool that increases lead conversions by 25% and I'd love to send it over to you, would you be the right person to send that over to?"

Something like this works for calls too.

"Hi there is that Sarah Harman? Sarah I understand that you're the marketing manager for AMTar. I've got a free tool that I'd like to send over which increases lead conversions by 25%. Would you be the right person to send that over to?"

- Is the person on the call the one who will benefit from the tool?
- Are they the person who will be buying it? (decision

maker, authority, purse string holder etc.)

☐   Are they the best person to continue building a relationship with?

Cold calls aren't a game of offering X products to Y people and seeing who buys. Cold calls and messages are about finding who the right person is and getting on a call with them. Notice how the message also doesn't ask for anything – it offers something. Two things in fact. It offers the benefit of increasing conversions and it offers it for free. If Sarah is the right person, we'll send that over and get some more information from her. We'll continue to build a relationship with her and we've identified that she is at least the most likely person in that company to talk to.

If Sarah says "no, I'm not the best person to send that over to" ask who is. Ask who you should be sending it to and if you can be put through to them, or get their contact information. At the cold stage, during qualification, the first question should always be "am I talking to the right person?"

Head over to sellfuturesnotfeatures.com/workbook for an example on how we generate leads and deliver killer content.

Plus, we'll send you the worksheets that accompany this book for free, straight to your email.

But Mike, I don't have a free tool?

Then build one. Or maybe don't be so literal? Create a report, process, diagram or guide. Training works-ish when doing cold outreach. But tools work 100x better. Head to sellyourservice.co.uk/outgrow for a brilliant free tool that helps you build tools with zero coding for your customers.

But can I guarantee something that increases conversions like that?

"Increase conversions by 25%" is the benefit. You need to choose a benefit that appeals to your customers and sounds like something they'd want. If you're selling financial advice, weight loss or industrial mining machinery then talk about what your customers care about and want.

What if I use this script and it doesn't work?

Tweak it and change the benefits and offer. DON'T think that it doesn't work because of the objective (finding out the right person to talk to) and start to try and sell. That's like realising your car is out of petrol and changing the tyres to make it move. Tweak the benefit and the messaging. Tweak the offer and the language. There are hundreds of options to choose from and you're going to have to test and experiment.

What if they take the tool, then what?

Give it to them, collect as much contact information as you can and offer the next stage – a full call or meeting. I always err on the side of motivated buyer and would rather assume the sale, than insist on due process. What I mean by this is that if I have someone take me up on the offer and ask for the tool, then I'll offer them the next stage too.

"Great! I'll send that over. Just so I have all the right information, can I get your email and phone number? If you like, we could get on a 15 minute call to talk through the tool, just to make sure that you get the most from it? How does 3pm tomorrow sound?"

The worst that happens is that they say no and just ask for the tool, you'll still get their information to follow up with. The best thing is that they say yes and you've got yourself a qualification call with the right person – nice work.

If they take you up on your tool offer, but turn down the call, the next stage is to get a call. Follow up, follow up, follow up.

But what if they've reached out to me?

Well this is great news! And it's the holy grail of inbound marketing. You have people discovering you and asking to talk to you! The process is still the same, you need to get on a call to qualify them and make sure that they're the right person to talk to.

If your cold outreach has agreed to a quick call, you're still going to qualify them and get some information out of them, namely the points we covered above. But I like to stick to BANTS to remind myself of what to ask.

BANTS

BANTS is a mainstay of sales and is almost certainly known by most salespeople. It's an acronym (yay) that covers the 5 most important areas of continuing a sale.

- ⬦ Budget
- ⬦ Authority
- ⬦ Needs
- ⬦ Timescale
- ⬦ Suppliers

What BANTS does for us is break down the questions that we need to ask any new lead or customer, before WE are willing to continue working with them. Remember the 5 questions before that we asked, to see if we really wanted to work with a customer?

1. They can afford to work with you
2. They can afford to put your advice into practice
3. You can help them get incredible results
4. You want to work with them/like them
5. They refer

BANTS is the framework for finding out if someone reaches those criteria.

Budget refers to the amount of money that they are willing and able to spend on this project. It's not just you they're buying remember, we want to get an idea if they can even afford what you're going to tell them to do.

Authority is asking who the decision maker and purse string holder is. Some people call these stakeholders, however I have found time and again that there are 2 people that matter and usually it's only one – the person who makes the final decision, signs off the invoice and pays for it.

Needs are the goals and requirements of the customer. What their problems are, what they're working with now and what their vision is for the project.

Timescale is when they're looking to start. Do not – and I repeat this – do not skip this question. This is basically asking "how desperate are they to fix the problem?" If they say they need this right now, that's urgency and demand. If they say "eh, we're evaluating a few options. We might start in the next few months…" that's a sign that they're not ready to buy.

Suppliers is asking who else they're working with, who else they're approaching and who is currently supplying their needs.

Example: sound-proofing a home office/studio.

Imagine you're an acoustics company that specialises in soundproofing and audio-dampening for home studios and offices. You transform home-work spaces into quiet areas and prevent noise leaking out into other areas of the home. Customers might include YouTube creators, podcasters, video editors, musicians and home workers with lots of meetings. Either through an advert or Google, someone finds you and sends you an email asking for a quote. Before you send one however, you need a little information about the project. So you book a call and call them up.

Sell Futures, Not Features

You: Hi there I'm calling from Acoustic Foam Ltd and wanted to talk to Mr. Killen about his recent request for a quote, to adjust the audio quality in his home office. In order to send you our most reliable and accurate quote, I'd need to ask a few questions if that's ok?

Customer: Of course, go ahead.

You: (Authority) Are you Mr. Killen?

Customer: Yes that's me.

You: (Budget) What's your budget?

Notice the short, direct and to the point question. Treat it like duct tape over a kidnapping victims mouth and rip it off. We'll cover this question in more detail later because it's where most people go badly wrong.

Customer: I don't know really. I suppose I'd be comfortable spending around £500?

You: (Authority) Great. And are you the final user and decision maker?

Customer: that's right, just me.

You: (Clarifying authority) Will anyone else be using the space? Do you have a partner or children that have any input?

Customer: No just me, I've been wanting to do this for a while.

You: (Need) Tell me about that, what are you looking to get done?

Customer: I want to sound-proof the room and prevent

163

noise from coming in too. It's not a noisy area I live in, but I have to be on podcast calls and interviews everyday, so I need to guarantee as much quiet as possible.

You: (Need) OK, what else?

Customer: Well I'd like someone to install it for me. I'm not good at DIY and would want some help.

You: (Need) OK great, what else?

Customer: I think that's about it.

You: (Need) Can I ask the dimensions of the room please? And would you be able to send over some photos of the space, as many as possible?

Customer: Sure it's 2m by 2m by 2m, I'll send the photos to your email.

You: (Timescale) Fantastic, thanks for that. And when are you looking to get started?

Customer: Sooner the better, if you had an appointment next week I'd take it.

You: (Suppliers) That's great news, I'm sure we can do something quickly. Can I ask if you're shopping around for quotes? And if so would you mind telling me who else you have in mind?

Customer: Yeah I've reached out to Quietfoam.com and Industrial Noise.

You: (Suppliers) What are you doing at the moment to adjust noise in your office and combat unwanted noise?

Customer: I've got a pair of noise cancelling headphones and a decent mic. But that doesn't really help with external noise when I'm on a call.

You: OK Mr. Killen, I'll get a quote sent over. Just a quick recap – you're looking to eliminate and reduce the unwanted noise into your office and studio, which is used only by you, so you can appear on calls and interviews without interference. You'd like some help setting it up and you have a budget of around £500, is that right?

Customer: That's exactly it.

You: Fantastic, I'll get that quote written up and have someone call you up to discuss it with you. Is next Tuesday at 3pm a good time?

Customer: Can someone just send the quote over?

You: Absolutely and we'll send it over. We've just found we can get things moving faster if we have an expert on the phone with you as we go through the quote, that way we eliminate back and forth and can get you set up faster. Tuesday at 3pm?

Customer: Sounds good, I'll speak to you then.

You: Thank you Mr. Killen, speak soon.

BANTS got us everything we needed. It's now up to us to decide if we want to continue working with Mr. Killen or not (I've heard he's really difficult to work with and insists on walking around in just his underwear). His budget might be a bit low to have someone both install the audio and supply the parts. Maybe this is a case of upselling the installation?

Or maybe and more likely, the customer doesn't need full soundproofing, which is very expensive and what he really needs is acoustic foam to dampen noise, which is a lot cheaper.

There are a lot of potential questions that come up during qualification like that, and it's important that at this stage, you DON'T answer them. I know it sounds counter-intuitive, but it's critical that we just qualify the customer and find out what we need. On the call, we could have explained that his budget is a little low for everything he needs. But that's ok, because we're going to do a sales call with him later and upsell him to a **more expensive package** that has everything he needs, while keeping it affordable.

On the call, he might have also asked about types of foam, systems to sound-proof things and other questions. Again, this is NOT the time to answer those questions. Right now we're just trying to figure out if we want the job. And although this might sound like it puts customers off, not answering their questions, it's a huge advantage. Why? Because you can easily hire people to qualify leads and get BANTS from them, without having to train them on sales processes or selling.

Customer: Can I ask if your acoustic foam is environmentally friendly?

Qualifier: Great question and to be honest I'm not the best person to ask. What I'll do is write that in the notes and make sure that whoever writes the quote talks you through that when we call. Did you have any other questions?

Customer: Can I ask another annoying and inane question?

Qualifier/you: Great question, right now I just need to get the basics from you in order to send over our best price and quote. I'll be sure to answer any and all questions you have a little later, is that OK?

Qualification calls are quick, to the point and focused. 99% of people also don't want to be on the phone. This is true of commercial and public sales. Selling to individuals or companies makes no difference, they're all trying to figure out the same thing.

Are you the best person to talk to? Should be we investing our time and resources into you? Can you afford us?

Make no mistake about it, the customer has researched you and qualified you already. And given the chance, some people just want to talk and talk and talk. Make sure they're worth working with if they have a habit of giving the Gettysburg Address every chance they get.

Getting a number

This is the most awkward part of the entire process and where most people fall down. Asking for the budget is a bit like asking someone out. You can beat around the bush and try to avoid the question, but the only way you'll know, is to ask. You absolutely have to ask for the budget. Have you ever sat down with a customer and presented the proposal to them, only for them to look at the price and say "oh we don't have that much. We were thinking $500 for the whole thing"? It used to happen to me a LOT. It's really disheartening to hear from someone that you're too expensive, or they didn't realise it would cost that much.

"I've asked around and that's easily over 10x what they charge"

"It can't cost that much! We only have $1000!"

"Our last website only cost us $1000!"

If you want to stop having these conversations, then you need to understand the customer's budget. However this can be a thorny subject for some people. Asking for the budget seems like a faux pas to many businesses.

They'll think I'm greedy

One of the most common reasons I hear businesses not asking for the budget, is because they worry that their customers will think they're greedy. The fear goes that if you ask someone for the budget, it'll appear like you are only interested in the money. I can understand that you need to make it clear that you're willing to help. You need to do everything you can, to assure the customer, that you've got their best interests at heart.

Sell Futures, Not Features

However this also should have come earlier in the process. If you're talking to a new customer, why are they talking to you? Surely there must be an element where they already trust you, or believe that you are going to help them? The fear that they'll think you're greedy if you ask in the budget, is no more true than you thinking they're selfish for wanting to improve their business.

The reality is that unless you know the customer's budget, you can't truly qualify them. How many of us have ever presented a proposal, only for the customer to say "I wasn't expecting it to be that much!"

Admittedly asking for the budget immediately, might not be the best course of action. It is in fact one of the first questions I ask, even if it's a brand-new customer who I've never interacted with.

"And what type of budget have you allocated for this project?"

I still get an enormous amount of tyre kickers, time wasters and people shopping around for a price. The reason I am able to command higher prices for my services, is because I don't entertain the idea of lower-priced services. If I have a brief discussion with them about starting a marketing campaign, improving some of their activities, or any other kind of work engagement. I want to know how serious they are. A business that quotes $25,000, is potentially someone I can work with. A business that quotes $1000 probably isn't someone I can help. The more you understand about the project, through qualification causing discussions, the better equipped you are to ask the budget question.

It also gives you a clear indication of what their expectations are compared to what they are willing to spend. Asking the customer about their budget, shows that you're serious about your business. There's not a huge difference between $10,000 and $12,000. There is an enormous difference between $500 and $25000.

They don't know

But what if they don't know their budget? Again this is probably an indicator that they are a new or inexperienced business. Every other purchase on the planet, from houses to cars to groceries, has an inherent budget allocation. In our minds where clear on what we are looking to spend for the everyday services that we consume. If I go into a restaurant and it's clear that breakfast is going to cost me £25, I'm either going to instinctively believe it's worth than or it's not.

For the record, The Rusty Pig in Ottery St Mary, Devon is absolutely worth paying £25 for breakfast.

For someone to not know what their budget is, to solve a problem they have, is an indication that they are either inexperienced or at the early stages of the project. It also means they probably haven't really thought about what it is they want from the project. They are probably just conscious of the fact that they want a new landing page and email sales campaign. A business that understands they want to generate $500,000 in revenue, will tell you that they are willing $150,000 to reach that number.

A business that doesn't know what their budget is, probably doesn't know what they would make if they were successful. We don't inherently exclude anyone who doesn't know their budget. But there are also a few key questions and tips, in order to get the answer out of them. Many times, they'll tell you they don't know, because they really don't want to tell you.

"We can't tell you"

Anyone who tells me that they can't tell me the budget, for a variety of reasons, is instantly a red flag for me. I've even walked out of meetings with potential customers because they've kicked up such a fuss about telling me the budget. You'll see just how awkward this really is (for them) when I tell you one of my budget asking secrets. There are a few reasons that people can't tell you the budget. I'll cover some of those below.

One of the main reasons is that they don't trust you. Ultimately, they don't want you knowing how much they've got to spend. Either because it's an exorbitantly high number, and they don't trust your ability. Or it's a ludicrously low number and they don't want to embarrass themselves. Anyone who flat out refuses to tell you their budget, walk away. Make it clear you only work with professionals, and professionals know their budgets.

"You'll just max out the proposal"

Another reason people are sometimes hesitant to give you a clear budget, is because they worry that you'll max out the cost proposal. I've got no idea why customers fear this. Or, why businesses think that their customers are worried about this. If you tell me your budget is $25,000, I'm going to attempt to give you $25,000 worth of value. Or would you rather have $23,000 worth of value, and $2000 change?

A budget is designed as the resources you are willing to invest, into YOUR OWN BUSINESS. If a customer isn't willing to divulge the budget, what they're really telling you is that they don't trust that you will deliver. Or, just as commonly, they believe that they aren't worth the investment themselves. I'm very hesitant to work with customers where their budget is everything they have. I'd rather work with a customer who has an allocated marketing budget, and our budget for the project, no matter how big, is just a part of that larger spend. Customers who have put everything on the line to work with you, are usually harder to work with. They're more likely to micromanage you and be breathing down your neck for the whole project.

If a customer refuses to tell you their budget, or they think you'll just max out the price on the proposal. Explain to them that it is your job to get the maximum level of return for the maximum level of investment. They shouldn't be afraid to tell you their budget, because of course your max out their budget, and you will do a great job because of it. However, as I mentioned, this thinking is usually an indicator that they don't have any more resources to spend. In my opinion, I'd walk away from this because it's likely they'll be a difficult customer to work with.

Stay quiet after asking

Here is my favourite tip about asking for the budget. Whichever of the questions that you use below (I've given you some examples on how to ask the budget below), make sure that after you ask the question, you stay totally silent. The only words that you want to hear out of the customers mouth, after you ask what their budget is, is a number and a currency.

What you are looking to hear is "we have a budget of $25,000". Or "we were looking to spend around $35,000". You are not going to accept "we were hoping you could tell us", "we have a number in mind but we're not willing to divulge it" or "I don't know, how much do you cost?"

All of those answers are extremely weak. The problem is as soon as they give an answer, we are often inclined to reply back. We'll usually say something like "that's fine" or "I'm sure we can talk about this later". Instead, next time, I want you to stay totally silent even after they give an answer. Unless they give you a currency and a number, that is a clear indicator of their physical budget, you do not say a word.

Is this awkward? Yes. Is it going to make your skin crawl? Yes. That's the point. You have made it clear, by staying silent, that they haven't given you the correct answer. By this point they will be desperate for your acceptance. They want to say something, in the period of silence, to break the tension. In reality, it will only be 3 or 4 seconds. But it will feel like an hour. Stay completely silent, until they give you a dollar and number figure.

Even if they keep talking themselves through it, or even if they stay silent while thinking, you stay quiet as well. Until they give you the answer you're looking for.

Do some maths

Another example is to run through some maths with the customer. If you're running a qualification call, you want to ask their goals and what kind of revenue they're hoping to generate. If they give you a goal that they want to generate $100,000, you can do some very basic maths, to work out a budget for them. I believe that a 1:4 ratio is perfectly acceptable as an investment towards of financial goal.

That means I believe for a $100,000 ROI, a budget of $25,000 is perfectly acceptable. In fact, depending on the customer, their situation and their resources, we might even increase that to 50% of their goal. Why so high? Well first of all I need the resources to be able to generate them a return. A 2:1 return on investment is still good. Doubling someone's money is better odds than you'll get at any casino. Also, if it's structured correctly, my marketing funnel should continue to generate them revenue long after I've completed the build. To invest $100,000 and to get $100,000 back including hundred customers who have spent $1000, you're essentially giving them hundred qualified, paying customers for free. Sounds pretty good deal to me.

If the customer genuinely doesn't seem to know their budget. Run through this maths in real time with them. Ask them if it sounds reasonable to invest $25,000 to get a $100,000 return. If they argue with you and say no. Walk away. Or have a bit of fun with them, and ask them which bank or investment fund they know of that will yield them a 4:1 ratio return on investment, and you'll go work for them instead.

Asking for the budget

Below I've got a few examples of how you can ask the budget, without coming across as greedy, and clearly making it obvious that this is an important question to you. The reason I like these questions, to get the budget is because it positions the customer as a serious business. A business that is unable to answer these questions clearly isn't serious about their own business. So why would they be serious about working with you?

Budget question example: What budget have you allocated for this project?

Straight out the gate, the easiest way to ask about the budget, is to ask about the budget. Don't add any frills, don't add anything after you asked the question (remember to stay quiet). When you're on the call with the customer and it's clear what their goals are, ask them what their budget is. You might already know their timescale, their previous suppliers, their need and the decision-makers. Now we just need to ask their budget.

95% of serious businesses, and serious customers, will be able to give you an answer straight away. No need to complicate it.

Budget question example: What are you willing to pay for these results?

If you're willing to ask the budget question after a qualification call. For example maybe you've needed to understand what the results are, and their goals are. A great follow-up question, is to ask "what are you willing to pay for these results?" What this does is position the budget question, as a question of investment. What are they willing to invest, to get the results that they seek?

176

Sell Futures, Not Features

Let's take the example of being in a gym. If you want to start losing weight, build muscle and get fit. What are you willing to invest to get those results? Depending on how strong your desire is, you might be willing to pay as high as $10,000 a year. But if someone was to reply "I have a budget of $25 a month", we know that the gym they're going to attend, isn't going to be as effective, or supportive. We must understand what they're willing to invest in their own business. And this is the budget.

Budget question example: What would achieving these goals mean for your business?

If I'm really struggling to get a budget out of the customer, and sometimes it's because customers are not very bright or quick. I might reframe the budget question. If we ran through the results that we had gathered from the customer, and their goals. It might look something like the below.

- ☐ $100,000 in revenue
- ☐ 100 customers at $1000 per sale
- ☐ 1000 new email leads

After it's clear what the measurable results are, I'll ask a bit of an open-ended question "what would achieving these goals mean for your business?" I want them to talk about the future of their business. And what this would mean for their business and life. If they tell me something like "this will give us an entirely new pool of customers to sell our services to." I know that the future benefit they are looking for, is a pool of new fresh customers, to upsell their high-ticket items to.

By asking what would achieving this goal mean, I'm opening up the idea that in order to get this we must make some kind of investment. If it's very clear that the need and the want is strong, a bit like our gym example above, I know that they've got a decent budget. And I want to find out what it is.

Budget question example: what do you think is reasonable to pay for that future?

Similar to the question above, we are reframing the budget question, as a question of investment. Businesses that aren't serious, or haven't thought seriously about this, will still try and talk their way around the subject. If they're not serious about their own business, they won't be serious about the budget.

Ask a customer their budget

My favourite part of this entire process, is staying quiet. In fact I use this technique in a lot of different questions. If someone has given me an answer which I don't find satisfactory, I'll stay quiet. Eventually their awkwardness will overpower them and they'll want to tell me the truth, or get closer to the truth. I understand that some of this might be very difficult and uncomfortable, but if you're serious about running a business that makes money, you must be willing to get out of your comfort zone. If you want to stop dealing with time wasters, tyre kickers and price comparisons. Get used to asking the budget question. Once you start doing that, you'll never go back.

Paid discovery/deep dive

One of the most profitable activities you can do when you've qualified a customer, is qualify them further but get them to pay for the privilege. That's right. Get the customer to pay you to tell them whether you will or won't work with them.

Deep dives or discovery calls or whatever you want to call them, are further explorations into the project and the customer. It might be asking them about their business, their life, their new project. But more importantly it'll be giving you access to all the information you need, to give them the best proposal or offer you can.

Example: Interior decorator

The customer is looking to redo their living room and dining room space. The interior decorator company has already been on a quick call to make sure they've got a decent budget and that the customer is looking to do work that the interior decorator can help with.

What the decorator then offers is a "Space Review". This is a deep dive of the room and a further qualification, at the customers expense. It's positioned as something like "What

I'd like to do is see the space and ask you a few further questions if that's ok? We have a Space Review process which makes sure that we get the best and most accurate quote to you, in order to cut down on too much back-and-forth. It's $997 for the session and will take roughly 2 hours. With that we'll create a full design outline which you can keep, even if you decide not to use us. If you do go ahead and use us we'll take that $997 off the final quote. Can I book you in for next Wednesday at 9am?"

Note that the close doesn't ask "if that's ok?" or "how do you feel about that?" It's a part of the plan, this is a standard process and the customer would be the strange one for not going ahead with it. There's a couple of other nice touches in an offer like this. First, we clearly explain that we'll reduce the price of the total project if they use us. So technically the Space Review is free. Secondly, we state that the brief report and proposal will be theirs to keep, meaning they can use it with someone else should they so desire.

A common mistake that a lot of people make, is not valuing their time. This goes as much for salespeople and business owners as it does for customers. Putting a price and a time on the meeting sets the stage and rewards you for your time. It's critical that we start to charge for things that cost us money. Even if you're a huge multinational corporation, small meetings and discovery calls should be billed. First of all, it's a more scalable method, second it qualifies out people who don't want to spend money and thirdly – people are more likely to buy the larger project from you when they've spent a little money.

If you're a small or micro business, this goes 10x for you too. You don't have the resources or budget to hire people and pay them while they waste time with low value clients. You need to find people who want to work with you and who can afford you. And as I mentioned, you're more likely to make the sale after you get the customer to run a paid discovery session with you. Discovery sessions don't have to be purely to qualify either. If you have a set price for your work and know what you want to charge, sometimes you need to just gather as much information as you can before you can start work. Artists for example know what they want to charge, and the more information they have the better. However it might be difficult to hand over a report or proposal if someone doesn't want to work with you.

Example: Pet portrait artist

You're a professional portrait artist who specialises in painting lifelike and striking portraits of people's pets. You charge £6000 minimum for the work. You receive an enquiry that someone wants a portrait of their dog. You've qualified them and understood that they have the budget and want to start soon.

Sell Futures, Not Features

"Hi there Mrs. Simpson. I understand you're looking to get a portrait done of your labradoodle, Fenton? Is that right? We run a Portrait Personality session where I get to know you, Fenton and really understand as much as I can about him and his personality. I've found that a 30-minute walk and then grabbing a coffee to ask some questions really allows me to give the best portrait I can and allows me to get lots of reference shots. It's £945 for the session where I'll ask lots of questions and take lots of reference photos. And if you decide to use me, that price is included in the portrait of course. And you can keep the photos too! Can I book you in for next Wednesday at 9am?"

The devil is in the detail and the more time and care and **attention you spend with your customers**, the more they'll be willing to spend. Notice how we got Fenton's name and made it about him? You need to be paid for your discovery time and research.

Here's what's really interesting – as an artist, you're probably going to work off one photo and most artists can do a pretty good job from one photo. However, what we have found time and again is that the customer is MORE happy with the final result when they perceive a high level of value and work has gone into the final product.

The discovery session for a project like this is mainly to understand the subject, get some photos and ask questions about the type of portrait the customer would like. Do they want it in a scene? Background or none? Do they have a reference photo to use? If not, would they like us to take one (for a further fee of course)? You can also get a sense of how… "particular", the customer might be. Listen to your gut and watch for red flags. If they seem difficult, then tell them you're too busy and refund the payment. Save yourself the hassle. Or be blunt with them, tell them that you'd think they'd be a difficult customer and thank them for their time.

The OTHER massive part of running discovery meetings like this is that the customer becomes invested because they've had to work on it. Asking questions about Fenton, his likes and dislikes, what stories she has of him and how she got him. All these types of questions allow the customer to talk, and the more they talk, the more bought into the product they are. A bit like how we eat with our eyes at a restaurant, there's a reason that "Burger: $5.95" doesn't sound as appealing as "Dry aged prime Aberdeen Angus beef served with heritage smooth cheddar and crisp farm fresh lettuce, topped with homemade spicy burger relish on a toasted brioche bun: $8.95" and you can charge more for it.

In the long run, the more time you spend diving into the project and getting to know the work and the customer, the better the results will be. And perhaps more important, the more bought in the customer will be.

When we run through the paid discovery, which I'll outline below, you might find that the customer isn't worth working with. The example of our pet portrait artist states that we're too busy and we'll refund the cost of the meeting. As a rule I try not to refund people after the sale. I'd rather offer them something else. But when it comes down to it, I'd rather give them their money back and tell them I'm just too busy. Be sensible and aware of your emotions. If YOU don't want to work with the customer after they've spent money on you, tell them that you're too busy and your schedule is too tight to work together. Refund them the meeting fee and move on.

How to run a paid discovery call

Let's now talk about a very high-level idea on how to run a paid discovery call. Whether business to business, or business to consumer, you want to spend time asking the right questions and STILL not answering customer questions – at least not yet.

I've found that paid discovery calls can last about 2 hours and work well in the morning. We'll also use this as an opportunity to sell them the larger project AND get them to write the proposal.

A paid discovery call is divided into 3 areas.

1. List of problems and goals
2. Understanding their resources
3. Asking if they want some help

184

Get a list of their goals

For some projects, this might seem more intuitive than others. For a website design project or an app, there will be a list of desires and goals that the customer has. For something simpler, there might not appear to be that many goals.

In my experience I've found that it has nothing to do with the project and is all about the customer – the individual human behind the project. One website project could have a professional and courteous person respond to the question "what are your goals?" with an answer like "we're looking to expand our market share and start to offer online products. We have revenue goals, needs and things we want to change" and they're willing to go deeper into each point. Others will respond with "I want a website" clearly having not given it much thought.

And the same for the pet portrait service. Some people will say "I want a commemorative portrait of my dog Fenton, whom I love dearly and I'd love to put it on my wall to remember him by." Others will say "I want a painting of my dog."

Your job is to take either response and continue to draw out the answers. We do this by asking 2 further questions:

- What else?
- Why is that important?

People have deep and underlying reasons for most of the

things they do. The more we can understand why they want a portrait, why they want a website and why they're taking this project on. People don't buy things to give you money. They buy things to spend money on themselves.

From golf equipment to kitchen knives, $40m worth of mining machinery to office supplies. The deep underlying motivation behind why someone spends money with you has more to do with themselves. And the further you can dig into that motivation, the more likely you are to make a sale.

What are your goals? What are you looking to achieve? What's the goal? Ask one of these or a variant of and get the ball rolling with what their goals are. Whether they state one or three or ten, keep asking "what else?" and get them to exhaust their list of goals. We want as much insight as possible.

After that, when we have an exhausted list all of their goals, we're going to dig deeper. My colleague and friend Troy from Agency Mavericks taught me this method. It's called "go wide, go deep". So far, we've gone wide with their list of goals. We've essentially listed a load of places all over the map that they want to go. Some might be similar and some might be close to each other, or even on the way to the next destination. Some will be on the other end of the map in the completely different direction. What we're asking for is a list of success points or indicators. Goals are basically "how do we know that we're successful" in a written format.

Next we'll go deep. This is where we find their underlying motivations and priorities. Listing out their goals and seeing them all written down will be very powerful for the customer. No matter what you're selling, an exercise like this gives clarity. From pet portraits to marketing strategy to mining machinery and sound proofing, seeing a list of all the things they want to accomplish is a strong value builder for the customer.

Going deep means asking "what's the priority? And why is that the priority?" Present the customer with the list of goals and ask them "above all else, which is the real priority here?" Then shut up and be quiet. Don't give examples or ideas, just be quiet. It might take them a minute or a second, but they'll tell you which of those goals is their core focus and that's where they want to go. It might have been the first goal on the list, but that doesn't matter. What matters is that they've connected with you on their goals. You've demonstrated that you've listened and you care about the project.

After they've told you their priority, lets dig deeper and ask "why?" Why is that goal the priority? What does that matter the most? Instantly the focus will shift from metric or objective based goals to emotions, feelings and deeper things which are important to the customer. Why one person wants their room sound-proofed is different to why someone else

187

wants their room sound-proofed. Why one person wants new mining machinery or a pet portrait, is different to why someone else wants it.

We're going to go wide again, asking for more reasons why that's the priority. Why? What else? Why else? This process is so revealing that many people start to uncover deeper motivations that they themselves didn't realise they had. You want a list of reasons why, as these are your motivations and sales points. While you might be delivering mining machinery or coaching or a portrait, what the customer is really buying is this deeper why.

Get a list of reasons why and then, we're going to go one level deeper. "Of all those reasons why, which would you say is the most important?" It might be that at this second level, most of the reasons why aren't very emotional or illogical. What we're looking for is deeper emotional and more human motivations behind getting the goal. The closer we get to the buyer's reason for doing anything, the better chance we have of making a sale. So get them to choose one "why" at the second level and then ask them again "why is that the most important?" We're going deeper into their motivation. Continue listing out reasons why that 2nd level why is so important. This will get us closer to the buyer and give us more insight as to why they're hoping you can help.

Everyone else will be selling portraits or machinery. You

will be selling success or memories or security. The reasons that people buy anything are always emotional. People don't buy cars and keyboards and holidays. They don't buy SIP-gates or websites or consulting. What they buy is success, confidence, sex, status and memories. They buy health and wealth, time, freedom and identity. Most artists are trying to sell paint and canvas, some artists are trying to sell the painting, you are going to sell the deep underlying motivation which drives their very personality. You're selling futures, not features.

Your list should look a little like this:

What are the goals for a new website?

- More leads
- More sales
- $400,000 in sales
- Increase revenue from $300,000
- Keep up with competition
- Give a better experience to the user
- Make the business more profitable ▢ Priority
    - o <u>Why is that the priority?</u>
    - o Expand the team
    - o Start to work remotely
    - o Revenue is good and growing
    - o But profit is getting thinner
    - o Cost of sales is going up

o Current advertising is becoming more expensive/less effective

o Don't feel the website is serving us as hard as it could

o Other businesses seem to make lots of money with their website

o We're not as profitable as we need to be

o I'm worried that we're in an unsafe position ☐ Priority

 ☐ <u>Why is that the priority?</u>

 ☐ One bad quarter and we could be wiped out

 ☐ I want to expand but also cover our bases

 ☐ I lost my last business to a lack of profits

 ☐ I want to change now while it's easier than leaving it

 ☐ My board and directors want more profit

 ☐ Unless we increase profits, we're in a risky position

 ☐ Our margins are thin now and its halting growth

 ☐ We need to protect ourselves from new competitors

 ☐ Our costs are likely to increase

 ☐ Feel a little unmotivated that we're

working so hard with little payoff
- ⯑ Want to reward the staff and team more
- ⯑ Grow to a position to sell (not that we want to sell) ☐ Priority
  - o I want to do more with the business
- ⯑ Feel proud of the website
- ⯑ Old designer has left
- ⯑ Feel it's time for an update
- ⯑ Increase our profile
- ⯑ Cut down on sales time
- ⯑ Offer more products
- ⯑ Make things more efficient

As you can see from the example above, the project moved from "wanting a new website" to "creating a business that's stronger". It moved from the feature of being a website (something replaceable), to the feeling and future of feeling secure (benefit). The emotional drive of protecting the business and securing the future is a very very powerful motivation.

Any sales message we give to the customer now is more than just a website, it's about securing their business and their future. That's one hell of a proposition and instantly raised your value (and therefor your price). Make no mistake, this process can be done with absolutely any and all products and services. Some require a deeper dive, some not so much.

You've heard the phrase "sell the hole, not the drill?" Well this is selling the satisfaction of hanging a picture on the wall yourself, your partner feeling proud of you and you displaying a picture you got for your wedding.

Get a list of their problems

Now we're going to get a list of their problems. This is a breakdown of everything they want to fix, change, edit, adjust, escape and remove. It's easier to find emotional language in the problems that someone faces, because we're better at expressing negative emotions. Negative emotions like anger, sadness and frustration are some of the first "languages" we learn. Happiness and joy and tranquillity are what we certainly aspire to, but many of us never learn to communicate our feelings beyond a form of anger or sadness.

We do the same thing as last time, go wide and go deep. Ask them for a list of their problems and what they're unhappy with. What would they fix or change if they could? What stresses them out? If you recognise some of these questions, great. That's because we're always focusing on the customer and the words and lexicon they use to describe their problems are exactly what you should be using in your sales messages and copy.

Same as last time, get a long list of their problems and then ask them "what's the priority?" Whatever they tell you, ask them why that's the priority and then "what else?" Why else is that the biggest problem on their plate? Once you have another list, get another priority. Of all those reasons, which one is the biggest reason? Ask for more reasons at this third level and you'll uncover more problems and emotions and more reasons for them to buy.

But what about consumers and individuals buying products like paintings or other decorative pieces? Instead of asking their problems, ask them about their worries or roadblocks. Why are they looking to buy now? Do they have any hesitations or concerns? What can they see going wrong with a purchase like this? The more fears you get out on the table, the more you can address them and close them on it. Ask them what's wrong with their current "set up?" Do they have a current painting or decoration which they don't like? Why don't they like it? If there isn't anything there right now, if the wall is blank so to speak, why is it blank? People buy things to solve problems, even things that seem deeply illogical, it's a problem in their mind.

Get the customer to tell you what they'll buy

Years ago I was selling a car contract to a woman who wanted a specific type of car. The car was as good as sold. But every option I presented to her v. I had a list of her goals and we hit every one of those marks. Clearly I was missing something. So I reversed the questions and started asking about her current car. What didn't she like about it? What was she frustrated by when she got in her car, when she drove it and parked it. It revealed an amazing, illogical and deeply emotional reason that she wasn't even aware of. The colour of the car wasn't important to her on her goals list. But after asking about her negative experiences she clearly hated black, blue, silver and white cars. Why? Because her ex-husband always had company cars and she was sick of those stock corporate car colours. She didn't want red, but she did want a car that clearly screamed "I am not my corporate husband." She even joked that I must think she was mad as a hatter for thinking this. I didn't think she was mad at all, if anything I thought she was now 5% more commission because most car colours cost a little more.

Now I knew I was selling an anti-husband. I was selling more than the features of the colour, I was selling what the colour represented. By the way, this is absolutely not a comment on women choosing the colour of a car over the features, or being more or less emotional than men. EVERYONE makes emotional buying decisions. I've had men insist on convertible model cars even though they are more expensive to insure, weigh more than their non-convertible counterpart and therefor cost more in fuel AND we live in England mate, you'll get to use it maybe 3 days a year.

Sell Futures, Not Features

The car colour was a feature, but it had to be translated into an emotion before it made sense to buy. Men make these bullshit claims just as much as anyone else. More horsepower, higher RPM for power tools. Material quality and grade for sports equipment. Whatever the product has, the feature represents an illogical argument that the customer has made internally to justify their purchase.

Armed with two lists, you now have a list of their problems and their goals. You're in a fantastic position to start making a sale and building a pitch for them. This relies on one of the most basic skills I rarely see people use – getting the customer to tell you what they'd buy.

Surely it can't be that simple? I'm afraid it is, it just relies on you asking them the right questions. What we've done here with a list of their goals and problems, is get them to tell you what they'd buy. They're not buying a website, they're buying financial security. They're not buying a car, they're buying "the hell with you and your new girlfriend". If we listen closely enough to the customer they will tell us exactly what they'll buy and what they want to spend money on.

Can't get in front of your customers for actual meetings? How can you get a list of goals and problems? Ask them via email, social, advertising and paying attention to data. If you publish 3 blog posts on 3 different topics and one clearly gets more views and engagement – that's your biggest problem/goal.

Email your customers asking them their problems. Email them asking for their goals and priorities. Get buyers to tell you what they'll buy. Once you have a list of goals and problems from the customer in real time, it's time for the offer and close. Repeat back their problems + Would you like some help with that?

Repeat back their problems

"So what it sounds like to me is that you're looking to secure the financial future of your business, to be in a 'saleable' position, but you don't want to sell. And currently your biggest problem is getting orders out on time. Does that sound right?"

Holy shit – the customer is thinking – this guy just read my mind.

In Maslow's hierarchy of needs, he places warmth and food and security at the bottom of the pyramid, with recognition and status at the top. It's an oversimplified model, but a pretty accurate one depending on the situation you're approaching it from. Because above all else, the #1 thing people want is to be in control. They want to be acknowledged, heard and accepted. Most frustrations and anger stem from not being heard and not being accepted, regardless of the circumstances. The reason people get pissed off with salespeople and sellers, is because the seller doesn't goddam listen.

When you repeat back using their words, the exact problem and statement that they've told you, you might think it's a simple act of repetition. You might even think it's almost cheating or manipulative. You might worry that they'll see right through it and call you out on it. "Yes – obviously I want that, I just told you!" But you'd be wrong. What you're demonstrating is that you care enough to listen and care enough to understand. You've acknowledged their problems and goals and in a totally non-judgemental fashion you've repeated back what they want, and you've even checked that you've heard correctly. You will instantly skyrocket to the position of trusted advisor and all you've done is ask questions.

First of all, you're essentially agreeing with them. Which again, a lot of salespeople have a habit of arguing with their customers. Both before and during the sale. You'll hear salespeople tell you what you want and what other people want. When you tell them a problem or a concern, they'll argue with you. Rule #2 of selling – agree with the customer. That's what "the customer is always right" means. It doesn't mean that if they demand free meals forever plus a private booth for cheap, that you have to give it to them. It means that they believe they're entitled to that. If they're right and you don't agree with them, you're wrong. In the customer's mind you're either with them or against them. So in listening to their problems you're repeating back the situation and you're agreeing with them.

Secondly, what people say usually isn't as calculated as you (or they) think. They have a whirlpool of emotions, thoughts and ideas in their head. Their mouth can only filter out so much. So even as they're speaking, they're thinking and feeling on the inside. I like to imagine it like one of those bingo ball machines spinning around with 100 colourful balls with numbers on them. When a ball is released, the machine knows that a ball is out and it vaguely knows what number, but it's also having to pay attention to the other 99 balls bouncing around. If you take the care and time to pick the ball up, hold onto it and repeat it back, it'll think you're doing a marvellous job. The person won't think you're just repeating back what they've said, they'll believe that you've been listening to them.

Finally, and this the most powerful part – you listened to them. Most people feel they are never heard or listened to. To really listen to someone and hear what they have to say, means to understand where they're coming from. This is why agreeing with the customer is so important, if you agree with someone, it typically means that you at least understand where they're coming from. It doesn't mean that you agree with their entire point of view, but you can at least find some common ground.

When you repeat back what they've told you, it seems like you've remembered what they've said and as a rule, we tend to remember things we find interesting. We also remember when people agree with us. We're demonstrating to the customer that we're on the same side as them. After you've repeated back their problems, you want to ask if you've understood them. "So it sounds like you want to [goal] and your biggest problem is [problem]. Does that sound right?"

Once the customer agrees with you, you're over the hard part. If they don't agree with you, it means you missed something. So go back and ask them what you missed. Repeat sections of go wide, go deep in order to uncover what the core sentence is. When you think you've uncovered it, ask again and make sure that they say "yes! That's it! You've got it!" Now comes the magic part.

Would you like some help with that?

This was taught to me by Frank Kern, who's an online marketing expert. He'd probably say he's terrible at sales but he's being modest. And one of the most powerful phrases I ever learned from him was asking "would you like some help with that?"

It's a tiny 7-word question that flips the model of selling on its head. Rather than asking if they want the product and if they want to buy, you're asking them if they want help. If they do want help, then they're now asking for your input. There's absolutely nothing wrong with asking people if they want to buy or asking them for the deal. For many of us though, having the customer ask you for help is a softer touch approach that often results in better conversions. Would you like some help with that? Yeah that'd be great!

It's a simple question and it leads into the final part of the sale, the close. You're putting the control in the hands of the customer. If they say they don't want help, then something somewhere has gone wrong. It's rare for someone to say "no", but it does happen, just not that often. When someone says "no" to being asked if they'd like help, it's usually because they're feeling a little out of control. I.e. they feel that the situation is maybe moving a little quickly or they aren't in full control. Saying no is the fastest way to get back in control of a situation.

We'll deal with objections later, but the first thing to remember is not to argue with the customer. If they say no, it's usually because they want to get back in control of the situation and saying yes might feel like giving up control. First, repeat the question with a bit more specificity, "ok, well would you like some help from me?" Sometimes being a little more specific and giving them time to answer the question yields a different result. The important thing is NOT to argue with them. Don't tell them that they do want to work with you. If they still say no, ask if they'd like you to leave or end the call. What we're asking them for IS a no this time. "No of course, not, don't leave. I just need some time to think."

When people are given the chance to say no, they feel more in control. I've only ever had one person say "yes" asking me to leave. I still to this day have absolutely zero idea what I did or why. Now that they've asked you to stay, listen to their objection and learn how to turn it. Let them air their worries and bring them back around. Then ask them again when they're ready, after you repeat the question would they like some help, and get them to say yes. It's impossible to sell something when people don't want it. They might need it, but unless they want it, you can't sell it.

Offer a solution

Now we offer them the solution, the next step. It's a simple process and people way way overcomplicate this. Think of offering the solution as providing directions. After they've said yes to wanting your help, say "Great! I think what's best is for me to take these notes and write up an action plan. I'll send it over in a few days, how does that sound?" You'd say something like that if you need to send a proposal or quote.

If you know exactly what the next step is, tell them. Rip that hostage tape off quickly. "Great! We have a 3-part workshop to develop your sales strategy. You get to bring your team and we'll build a plan that starts to move you towards a better sales process. It's $14,000 for the 3 days and we'll take care of the location and refreshments. We can take payment by card or transfer."

This is the stage that matters, this is the part of the process that counts. You could have the most insightful and powerful discovery session of all time, but unless you move them to that next stage, it's all for nothing. Yes, the customer has paid you for this, but you need to play a bigger game. What's the bigger picture? What's the end game? You have to be crystal clear on what you want the customer to do next, because they sure as hell aren't.

Remember, they've asked for your help, they have asked you to help them. They're looking to you for the next stage. They might balk at the price or ask for a discount or throw up their arms. But you won't know unless you ask.

Most people don't get what they want, because they don't know what they want. The 2 key components to a successful pitch/negotiation are:

1. Know what you want

2. Make sure the other side knows what you want

The strategy discovery type session I've outlined about is so powerful, because most people being asked these questions don't really know what they want. When it becomes clear to them what they want and it is clear to them that someone else understands what they want, it's like a weight lifted from their shoulders.

There are few things worse than a salesperson who doesn't know what they want the customer to do. You could be the world's greatest artist, photographer, designer, solicitor, chef or musician. But no customer is going to do your selling for you. We tend to shy away from asking for the deal because we're worried what will happen. We believe that if we just show enough skill and "be there", that'll be enough. And it's wrong. It doesn't lead anywhere.

Have you ever been in a meeting where you were being sold to, and on some level you knew what the next stage was? I.e. you need to pay them and hand some money over. But for whatever reason the salesperson had skirted around the issue and made excuses or never just SAID what the next stage is? I have – in fact I've been that salesperson. It's painful to watch on both sides. And what I've learned is that I'm better off starting with telling the customer what I want them to do, them thinking "that's never going to happen" and winning them over. Never telling them what I want is the first step towards never getting it.

I believe that the world would be a much better place if people were more open about what they want. Not letting people try to guess what they want, for fear of offence. Most negotiations fail because one or both sides don't really know what they want the outcome to be. Second to that, they fail because they never tell the other side what they want.

When do you ask for the deal?

"No one ever lost a deal by making an offer too early. You will only ever lose a deal by offering it too late." Unknown

One of the most common questions I'm asked is "when do you ask for the deal?" Surely you need to build a relationship, nurture the customer wait for the right time to ask them to buy from you? My advice is always the same, no one ever lost a deal by making an offer too early. You will only ever lose a deal by offering it too late. The worst that will happen if you offer a product or service too quickly or too soon, is the customer saying "no", and you can ask why. When you wait for the "right moment" and miss the sale because someone else got in before you, you won't have the chance to ask "why didn't you buy from me" because the answer will always be "because you never asked." When it comes to sales, you either need to be the first person to talk to the customer, or the last.

Offer to help as soon as you can. Make sure you have some clue as to what they want and offer to help. No normal person is going to balk at the idea of you charging for your help. If they say no, ask why and turn them. But you never know, some of them might just say yes.

One of the worst things to come out of email and marketing automation is the "nurture sequence". The idea is that once you get a lead, you need to develop a deep relationship with them by sending a long sequence of educational emails to them before you can make a sale. This principle however was bastardised by people who want to avoid ANY sales. The idea of selling, closing, pitching, turning objections and facing rejection is so terrifying to them, that they'll come up with long elaborate email sequences to put off making a sale. It's called A.B.S. and everyone falls for it. Doing work that looks like it leads to sales, but really it's a method of procrastination.

Does email marketing work? 100%. It's our most profitable and high returning marketing activity and asset. Does nurturing work? Absolutely – when done correctly. Don't fall into the trap of thinking that sending 34 emails to someone is going to magically convert them into a customer – it won't.

We often hear of the analogy that selling is a bit like dating. You might know that you want to close someone on the big deal, but that's like proposing on the first date. Instead, you need to get their number, go on a date and build it naturally over time. But you still need to ask them on a date. You have to do something which could result in rejection and a little humiliation. You can't nurture someone to marriage. You have to take those risks and close those deals. Nurturing comes during the relationship, not before it. When I first met my wife Olivia, she was out with her mate and she was absolutely not looking to "meet" someone. We had a mutual friend in common and after a few drinks at a pub we moved onto a club and started talking. Eventually, I asked her out and her first words were "that took you long enough!"

She joked to me that she was clearly interested. She left her mate with some other friends to go off and talk with me (we were both dirt poor and had just been made redundant, so we shared a water). Clearly she wasn't in it for the free drink. What more could she have done to show me she was interested!? It seems obvious now but back then, in that night, I was trying to nurture a date out of her. When really, telling her what I wanted was a much easier and clearer route. There's nothing more frustrating to a customer than someone who refuses to sell to them. Ask early, make mistakes and learn to read the signs. Because they're there and buyers want to buy.

Make sure to get our Qualify Cheatsheet plus 8 other worksheets at sellfuturesnotfeatures.com/workbook. We'll send you the worksheets that accompany this book for free, straight to your email. Plus some extra bonus training that only readers of this book can access.

Summary:

☐ Focus on making sure that they are the right customer for YOU before you launch into selling

206

- It's better to have an awkward conversation about money and price BEFORE you invest any time and resources into making the sale

- You can sell a second, deeper qualification under the guise of discovery or an audit or deep dive, which pays you for your time to uncover if they really are a customer worth working with

- Unless you know exactly which type of customer you'd love to work with, and who you'd turn down, you'll always be at the behest of working with whoever comes your way

Chapter 6 - Sales messaging and selling

Sales copywriting scales conversations you've already had

Imagine hiring a salesperson who delivered the perfect, mistake-free, high-energy pitch 24 hours a day to anyone and everyone who they saw. No matter what time of day or night, whether it was one person or 1000, they sold a product in the exact same way to the same high standard over and over, with zero change in their delivery.

This is the dream salesperson for many businesses and perhaps even the dream partner for many salespeople. And through the use of sales copy, you can create such a sales team. When I first started my business Sell Your Service and even before that with my first marketing agency, it was clear that I couldn't have as many conversations as I wanted. There simply wasn't enough time in the day to speak to all the people I wanted to. Besides that, it wasn't a good use of my time, as many people would be unsuitable for further projects. The problem then became "how can I scale the number of sales conversations I'm having with people, while at the same time reducing the number of low-quality leads and only focusing on the high-quality leads?"

Sell Futures, Not Features

To many, the solution would have been to just work more hours or keep doing what they were doing. But I knew that I needed a different approach. Which is when I took a proposal that had converted and worked well, for a project that I wanted to replicate with other customers, and I published it. At the time, this was for my marketing agency, and I didn't really know what I was doing. I just figured that if a proposal with benefits, pricing and timescales that converted was out there in the public view, it might attract people who wanted the same process. Lo and behold, what I had created was my first sales letter.

Anyone even mildly interested in talking to me was shown this page. If I went to networking events or talks, I would tell people to go to that page on my website. I had essentially taken the copy from that proposal and turned it into a webpage on my site. I could now show as many people as I needed what I could do, and they would either want to buy, or not. Now of course this page didn't convert at a high percentage, but it did free up my time massively. As anyone who wanted to work with me could read in plain English what they'd be getting from me. No fluff or bullshit. Simply by using that page, we did convert a few new clients, but I wondered if I could make it better.

Proposals suit a certain stage of the buying process, they're not brilliant at introducing the service to the customer.

They're more suited to closing and exchanges, but having it on my site was still 100x more effective than having NOTHING. And what was really interesting is that it still converted more customers than my standard "service offering" style pages that told customers what we did.

The difference is that the proposal sales page was selling the customer, not the project. Because it was for a real customer, it spoke to their problems and goals and desires. Because it was focused on them, it became less about me and the service, and more about them and their life. When I published it, I made it anonymous, but the story still remained. I didn't have a long list of complex marketing terms and products. The cost and timescale pages were very simple.

- Website design and development
  - 10 weeks
  - $15,000
- 6 weeks internet marketing coaching
  - 6 weeks
  - $5000
- Email marketing automation
  - 8 weeks and ongoing
  - $5000 setup
  - $1000 per month going forward

Many people believe that the proposal needs to have lots of wording around the product, but it doesn't. Most of the copy in the proposal talked about the problems the customer had, what their goals were and what they'd tried before. It talked about their fears and worries as well as what their market and competition were doing. And this was 100x more interesting to any reader because it spoke to and about, them.

When I published the proposal, I didn't realise that I was doing something which sales copywriters had been doing for decades. They were taking conversations that worked and had gone well in the past, documenting them and publishing them. If one person wanted a product because of the story they had, then surely others would too?

This blew my perception of what sales could mean to my business, out of the water. Video, podcast, sales letters, emails, social media, blog posts, web pages, online adverts – they could all take a message from a successful sale and scale it infinitely. Over and over someone could read the same sales message and get the same delivery as the next person, for a few pennies a month cost to me.

Sales copy scales conversations that you've had, and replicates them. There's even evidence to suggest that sales copy can even outperform a person, because of the consistency and comfort of consuming sales copy on the customer's own time. Imagine knowing that you could pitch to your customers in their home, or their office. And even better? THEY invited you in!

Sell Futures, Not Features

Over the years, I worked on my sales copywriting over and over. I also worked on my sales principles for face-to-face work, video pitching, webinar sales, audio sales, live seminars in person and one on one sales calls. Phone, Zoom, Skype, letters, books, pages – every method of communication out there became a platform for me to test, tweak and replicate a sales message. If I found one that worked, I'd capture it and push it out on other platforms that didn't need me to deliver it. This entire chapter is dedicated to the act of the sale, sales messaging (what the customer hears about what you're saying – often two different things) and sales copy. I want to help you crush your face-to-face sales, in order for you to replicate the results on an evergreen platform. The method you'll learn to sell face to face, one on one, is exactly the same as the method for writing sales letters, filming sales videos and creating ongoing sales collateral, the way the customer consumes/ watches/ sees/ listens is all that changes.

Writing lots of sales copy and content can be a bit of a drag. If you head over to sellfuturesnotfeatures.com/workbook you can download our entire 9 part workbook for free to make sure you don't miss anything.

We'll send you the worksheets that accompany this book for free, straight to your email. Plus, you can follow the exercises along in this book and be one of the action takers.

Sell the person, not the pen

Blair Warren, an expert copywriter, has a list of five things that people need to hear from salespeople in order to buy. Most people believe that benefits are just "good things that the product does" but it's far deeper than that. Benefits expose truths about the customers life and how they live. They take them on an emotional journey and pull/push between desire and escape. Your solution needs to stir up the status quo and demonstrate that things can be better.

In the film The Wolf Of Wall Street, Leonardo DiCaprio plays Jordan Belfort as a guy who cons people out of money. Since coming out of prison Jordan has made a living as a sale's motivational speaker. One of the famous scenes in the film and book is when he asks people to "sell me this pen."

Sales trainers and managers LOVE this question and it's a classic tool to see where people are in their sales journey. Sales managers especially love this question because it puts people on the spot. However, both sales managers asking the question AND salespeople answering the question miss the point.

When I first went to university, I needed a job because chicken wings, weed and sambuca weren't going to buy themselves. I got a job at a high-end high-street retailer called John Lewis. For those who don't know, John Lewis is an upmarket high-street department store. We had to wear a suit and tie to work there (although I'm not sure that's the case anymore) and their hiring policies were very strict. As I had sales experience, I figured I was a shoo-in. I had previously worked for their food and grocery shop, Waitrose, so I knew to wear a suit to the interview, speak well and not get drunk the night before. As we were ushered through to the training room, we were split into groups of around 10 people and the interview/training began. Most people wore suits or at least smart clothing, but my eye was caught by a scruffy long haired guy wearing trainers and torn jeans.

I'm ashamed to say I immediately judged this guy, around my age and thought "he obviously isn't getting in. What a joke. Wear a suit man!" We went around being asked the same kinds of dumb questions that companies and HR departments love to ask. "Tell us something interesting about yourself. What's your biggest strength? What's your biggest weakness?" And then they handed out a pen and asked us to "sell the pen" to the group. I watched the pen make its way around the group and eventually the scruffy haired guy (Tom as I later learned), picked it up. Tom stood up and asked "does anyone have a pen?" A few people put their hands up, but most didn't. "I work at a club in town and I can get you in for free tonight with drinks if you write your name and number down on this card."

People looked around and realised they couldn't write their

name and number without a pen. "If you need a pen" he continued "I've got one available for £5." My jaw was wide open. This guy didn't just play the exercise, he literally sold the pen. A few people tried to be clever and borrow pens from other people, but it was clear to me and the hiring manager that he absolutely understood the sales process. My pen selling technique was exactly the same as everyone else's, I talked about the pen. Tom talked about the person buying the pen. A few months later, Tom and I became good friends and eventually housemates. I learned a lot about advertising, messaging and most importantly, making the customer feel good about their decision.

The point is NOT to sell the pen. The point is to sell the person. In Wolf Of Wall Street, Brad (played by the ludicrously handsome Jon Bernthal) explains that it's about creating demand. You must create demand to sell the pen. And what most people misunderstand is that demand isn't created by how good the product is, it's created by what the customer wants. Most salespeople will launch into a diatribe about how good the pen is or talk about a specific feature. Some will jokingly try to sex up the pen and overly sell it (which is really just the same as talking about the pen). You don't buy a pen to write, you buy a pen to capture something of value. You don't buy a bed, you buy a better night's sleep. You don't buy lingerie; you buy escapism and fantasy. You don't buy features, you buy futures.

So how can you sell a pen? In this exact example, depending on who the customer is, we need to tap into something they want. Do they want Megan Fox's phone number? Or do they want a recipe for chocolate cake? Do they want to write down the address of a private members club? What if they want to draw out a map to buried treasure? The creation of demand is entirely in the mind of the customer and that's what we're exposing. And Blair Warren has 5 areas that he likes to identify in order to expose those demands. These 5 points uncover what the CUSTOMER wants.

- ⬜ Confirm their suspicions
- ⬜ Quell their fears
- ⬜ Justify their mistakes and failures
- ⬜ Believe in their dreams and goals
- ⬜ Fight their enemies and battles

These 5 areas are items that people are looking for in a relationship. And make no mistake that the sale you're making comes off the back of that relationship. When you're looking to make a sale, for undersea mining machinery, stationary or software, the buyer is looking for these areas to be covered by you.

They might not know they're looking for them, but they are.

Confirm their suspicions

Sell Futures, Not Features

Everyone has their suspicions and theories on why their life is the way it is. Everyone has thoughts and beliefs about the world and what's happening, or justifications as to why they've made the choices they have. And there is nothing sweeter in the world than hearing that you were right all along.

In order to get from where they are now, to where they want to be, customers need to undergo a transformation. As we've covered before, it's the transformation that they're really buying. But, there is a massive roadblock between now and then. That roadblock is their own internal limiting belief or beliefs. They have suspicions that it's been difficult in the past for them because of X, or that other people have it easy because of Y. Or they believe that everyone else has what they want because of Z.

If you've ever felt that advertising on Facebook is difficult, you're right. Because Facebook doesn't want small businesses advertising on there, it wants larger corporations like Coca-Cola and Disney. So it doesn't make it easy for small businesses, that's why you've been struggling in the past.

If you've ever felt that the diets and meal plans you've bought in the past don't work, you're right – they don't. If you've ever thought that you seem to put the weight on as fast as it comes off, for every new diet, that's because diet companies don't want you to lose weight – because then you're no longer a customer.

If you've ever felt that only rich people can afford property to rent out, you're right. The rich get richer but there IS a way to get on their level without loads of spare cash in the bank.

See how each of these suspicions play out in the customer's mind? When we agree with them, we show them that we're on the same side. Rule #2 of sales, agree with the customer.

Quell their fears

Fear is the great motivator, so they say. However it works both ways. Motivation can force us to act but it can cause us to remain still. Your customers, ALL your customers, no matter who they are, have fears. From new parents to professional athletes, to multi-billionaire CEOs and struggling entrepreneurs, all have fears. Fears are very human and they're an important part of our life and personality. But fears are also usually, totally illogical.

Coldly and bluntly, most humans as a percentage have very little to fear. You're probably not going to die and you're probably not going to experience a tragic and traumatic event. The thing that you're worrying about probably isn't going to happen. And if it does, then there isn't anything you can do about it anyway. And if you can do something about it, then you needn't worry at all. BUT we don't think like this when it comes to our unique situation. Because our fears are more real and more obvious. People just don't understand what it's like to be you and have your life. Your fears matter. And that is the key component to great sales.

When you side with your customers and understand their fears, you're showing them that you care. Think about when you were a child, the things you worried about paled in comparison to what you are afraid of today. But that doesn't make them less real or less scary. And, the parent or teacher or guardian who calmed you down and listened to your fears, how did that make you feel? It makes you feel like you've shared your problem, like someone else understands and you've been heard. If you can understand what your customers are afraid of, you can understand what their motivations are and that is what drives action and sales.

It's also worth noting that your customers aren't afraid of living a life without new mining machinery or server racks. No one wakes up in the night, sweating and worrying, thinking "Christ, I need to find a marketing consultant – quick!"

People lay awake thinking "my father was right, I'll never amount to anything" or "if I die tomorrow, no one will miss me." **Deep and dark fears are what lay in the heart of** all people, no matter if you're selling pens, vaccines or jet engines, the person you're selling to is making decisions which either relieve those fears or put them at bay. In your sales copy and talk, it might be a bit direct and weird to start by saying "I know what you're thinking, that your life will amount to nothing", but you do need to quell and quieten people's fears.

They have fears of failure and of success. They have fears of trying and looking stupid and getting it wrong. They're afraid of buying your products and making the wrong decision. Will buying this and taking this action come back and bite me in the ass? Within your sales copy you need to do two things:

1. Quell their fears about buying the product
2. Show that buying this product will help them with their other fears

Fear is a powerful motivator, but it can also motivate people to hold onto their money. More than anything, when people buy something, they just want to feel good about the decision they're making. That's about as complex as it gets.

Justify their mistakes and failures

Nothing is sweeter to the human ear than "it wasn't your fault." Again, this isn't a case of either agreeing with the customer or even letting them get away with something. It's about showing them that you understand their situation.

A few years back I lost a customer $60,000 on online advertising. I was brash, arrogant, and not paying attention. Within a month, I lost them $60,000 and of course they were furious (and rightly so). At the time I had loads of excuses and reasons why it didn't work out. I could blame loads of other people and events and even the advertising platform. Deep down, I knew it was my fault, and that prevented me from using paid online ads for a while. Because I was terrified of making the same mistakes (fear) and worried it would happen again.

The process that got me around to using online ads again, wasn't through telling me how amazing they were and how much money they could make. Internally, I was saying "yeah I've heard this all before, the potential win isn't worth the humiliation of failure. I've tried all this before and it didn't work" (loss aversion). The process that worked was the course teacher telling me "I know how you feel. I've wasted money on ads and it hasn't worked for me either. Guess what, it's not your fault. You were taught the wrong things and destined to fail."

This person was selling me a course and training, but rather than telling me how much ROI they made through ads, they were telling me that my past mistakes weren't my fault. They were allowing me to justify my mistakes and failures. Whether or not you take an "extreme ownership" position in mistakes and failure, or whatever your feelings on mistakes and failure, it's still nice to hear someone be on your side (note how often that phrase comes up – on your side), not

221

blame you and still want to talk to you. "It's ok, it's not your fault." Even if you do think it's your fault and even if it IS your fault, having someone allow you to take it easier on yourself is a huge relief for people.

Customers might have tried the same thing before, but got it wrong. Or tried something completely different to get to their end goal. Either their method is wrong, or the choice of action. If you can side with them and explain that you don't blame them or judge them, they're more likely to listen to you and see you as on their side.

Believe in their dreams and goals

In The Simpsons episode "You Only Move Twice", Homer works for the charming and welcoming (not to mention a personal role model of mine), Hank Scorpio. Evil genius and global terrorist, Hank asks Homer what his dream is. Homer replies that his deepest dream is to own the Dallas Cowboys.

"I bet people laughed at you when you told 'em that dream. Homer, don't give up. They laughed at me the first time I wore jeans with a sport coat."

-Hank Scorpio

The reason I love this quote and absurd statement, is because Hank understands the key to motivating people to join him, making decisions and growing a relationship. Believe in their dreams and goals, and never ever laugh when someone tells you what their dream is. The brutal reality is that most of us either never have a large dream, for fear of telling people and getting laughed at. Or we keep it to ourselves for the same reason. Most of your early education is spent telling you what you could become. Then your latter part of education tells you what you will become. Ideas above your station, sticking your neck out, be happy to settle – these are all statements from people who don't want you to succeed or surpass them.

When someone like you listens to other people's dreams and goals, and rather than laugh or tell them "it'll never happen", you ask them how you can help. You become a very different type of supplier. Someone who believes in the goals and dreams of another person is INFINITELY more interesting, magnetic and inspiring than someone who tells people to "aim lower". Does that mean that every mental and huge dream of your clients is going to happen? Almost certainly not, and the fact remains that most people never will achieve their dreams for hundreds of reasons. But that's not for you to decide or say, your job is to take their dreams of spending more time with their family, retiring at 40 or sailing around the world and responding with "how can I help you make that happen?"

The benefits exercise we did earlier will tell you many of the dreams that people have. Status and moral goals are closely tied to dreams, with most people wanting freedom, respect and an easier life. It's a big risk telling someone your dreams, because we all fear being made fun of. Having a dream is essentially saying "I think things could be better." Some people are happy with where they are, some aren't. When someone announces a dream, they are directly stating that the current status quo is not where they want to stay. This could be seen as offensive or even arrogant by some people, but that's their problem. You on the other hand are going to write about, encourage and believe in their dreams and goals – it'll set you apart extremely quickly.

Fight their problems and battles

All five of these statements could really be summed up as "be on their side". The final part of this process is to fight their problems and battles. Blair Warren calls this throw rocks at their enemies. Who ISN'T on their side? Who is the person or company that makes their life difficult? Nothing binds people together faster than a common enemy.

This is not only about addressing the same problems and recognising the same headaches, but also about literally finding an enemy together who you can vanquish. Combined with the wrong information they've been given before AND their suspicions, we should be able to find a common enemy that we want to eliminate. If this sounds a little aggressive, you need to know and accept that you need to be aggressive.

You are the leader on the front line, you're the chief at the start of battle, rallying the soldiers. You are willing to stand up and tell other people that this is unacceptable and you're not going to stand for it any longer. If you want to get people on your side, be on their side.

The problem and enemy that you're facing will come in one of two types.

1. Literal

2. Conceptual

Literal problems and enemies are people, places, things and companies. They're things you can point to and even touch. Terrorists are an enemy; they are a problem. Billionaire hedge fund managers. Bullies, Amazon, Walmart, Martin Shkrekelikilikji. These people are to some, the enemy. They're tangible and literal figures that represent the problem or even cause the problems that your customers are facing. Cheap competition, online scams, hype-marketers, pharmaceutical businesses. If they have a name and an address, you can point a finger to them and say "that's the enemy, we're going to fight them." ·

Conceptual enemies are ideas, events, results, beliefs and situations. Weight gain, debt, self-confidence, communism, capitalism, 2-day weekends. These are ideas and beliefs that people and groups have, but that don't really "live" anywhere. You can find evidence of them but you might struggle to point them out. However, conceptual problems and enemies are probably more powerful than literal enemies because they are deeper more emotional struggles that people have.

Even better is when you can combine a literal enemy and a conceptual enemy. If your literal enemy is a believer in a conceptual problem (or they promote/exacerbate it), you've got a winning battle cry.

Why are you miserable and unhappy? Because Kelly from accounts (literal) is a killer golf player and she beats you all the time (conceptual). Because Jeff Bezos and Amazon (literal) are putting hard working small businesses like you out of business (conceptual). Because cheap competitors from overseas (literal) are forcing you to lower your prices and lose customers (conceptual).

Being the standard bearer and identifying the enemy is a solid and clear platform to drive sales. If you can identify one literal enemy (who also happens to have fed them the wrong information and who your customer has suspicions over already) and three conceptual problems – you are onto a winner.

Offer a solution

"Don't come to me with problems, come to me with solutions." Unknown

I see a lot of great sales copy, offers and pitches fall down at the last minute because…they don't offer a solution. Many

226

salespeople believe that just because their cause is strong enough and they've aligned with their reader, that the solution is obvious. It isn't – ever. You need to make the solution HYPER specific and actionable. WHAT is the next step? What is the solution? This comes in two parts.

1. The call to action (CTA)

2. The Method

The call to action is the literal action that someone must take to go to the next stage. Sign here, pay now, pay a deposit, click this button, sign up here. It's the physical action that they need to take next – without question this is the most important part of the process. Forget this and you might as well not write anything. I've seen pitches, proposals, sales videos, sales letters, adverts, offers and seminars fall completely flat because the sales person doesn't give a specific CTA.

The method is the "how" before the result. It's the method that the salesperson or team or company uses to fix problems, reach goals, realise dreams and fight enemies. It's the system that fixes mistakes, makes sure they never happen and gives your customer the much-needed advantage. The problem is that too many people get "The Method" wrong.

First, they explain the method too early. Second, they explain their operations process, rather than the "method". The first problem is easy to solve, bring up the method later in the process. The mistake is thinking that people want to learn how to fix their problems and they do...just not yet. Think of the method or solution as eating a cake, you need to bake the ingredients first – problems, mistakes, suspicions, enemies and dreams.

The second problem of The Method is when salespeople mistake their operation procedure for what people really want to read. A classic sign of selling features rather than futures. You have a method, no doubt, for solving your customer's problems. However, your method isn't what the customer is going to experience. More importantly, we want to show off some more benefits and futures that they'll experience along the way.

The way you need to think about The Method, is to think about what you'd tell the customer to do even if they didn't buy from you. If they wanted to totally go this on their own, what would they need to do? Don't make the mistake of making the process sound overly complicated or difficult. That will only serve to put the customer off. It might sound counter-intuitive to offer a solution to their problems without you at the centre of it, but that's just it. It's not about you.

The Method that you demonstrate to the customer needs to be something they can understand. You might take for granted your own insider knowledge. Surely everyone knows what macros are, right? Obviously the customer will know what a

hot-swap is. Just tell them to set it up with their email client –
it's easy. Except, it's not easy. The customer has no idea what
the hell you're talking about. The method that you tell the
customer needs to be something which they can understand
and even DO without you. YOUR job will be to tell them
afterward "and if you want some help with that, we can do all
that for you."

Let's look at two different methods. One is from the
perspective of the business or salesperson. The other is from
the perspective of the customer. Some of the differences
might be subtle, but some will be glaring and obvious. What
we're trying to do with the method is explain a process which
is so simple, that a child could understand it. The problem
we're trying to solve is sending an email – a very simple but
specific problem.

Salesperson/businesses method	Customer's method
▪ Open your email client ▪ Locate your address book or copy and paste the email address you're looking to send in the "To" field ▪ In the text field, write the main message ▪ Decide on using a read receipt or not ▪ Press the send button ▪ Exit the application	▪ How – how will you send your email? Do you use Apple Mail, Gmail, Outlook or something else (called an email client)? ▪ Who – who are you sending an email to? Do you have their address already or are you replying to an email? You'll need their email address which usually looks like username@company.com ▪ What – what's the message? Use the large text box to write your message, including your name, and theirs at the top. ▪ When – when you're ready to send, give it a once over and check for mistakes, then click send.

Again, to most people reading this book, the left column probably gives as much information as you need. But your customers might not be you. They might need a simple breakdown of each stage so they can learn through this process. Creating solutions like the right-hand column is far more appealing to the customer. Your method needs to be specific and easy to understand. When you can break down something as simple as email, into a method that makes sense to the user, you're increasing your authority in their eyes.

Designing marketing campaigns, logo design, installing mining machinery, building a table, losing weight, gaining self-confidence. Any and all problems need to be broken down into a method that the customer can understand. A plan that they can follow. And when you offer to work alongside them to deliver that method, it's an obvious win.

Sales letter

I want to talk now about structuring a pitch, sales letter or even a proposal. This is basically the content that you'll give to the customer, to make your case that you're a good person to work with.

This structure is something I call "The Sales Letter", but could easily be a webpage, a video, a live in person pitch, a phone call, a Zoom call, a webinar, training seminar, proposal, written sales page or any other time you're trying to convert someone from "interested" into "buyer". Don't

231

overcomplicate the messaging and don't overcomplicate the delivery. If you can use these same prompts or beats, and follow this structure, you'll be able to make 3-minute sales pitches and 45-minute talks. Just in the same way that novels turn into films and then into TV series' and back into novels, the structure or journey of the listener (your customer) is pretty much the same.

The most common mistake people make when in sales messaging mode, is trying to head straight into the meat. They dive straight into the features and the pricing because they believe that's what the customer wants. Hell, sometimes the customer believes that's what they want. But just like at Easter when I believe I want nothing more than a diet of chocolate eggs and Jelly Baby Chicks – someone else knows better and it'll overwhelm me if I do just that.

You've got everything you need to create a killer sales letter. Use this as your pitch, sales copy, emails, webinars, videos, brochures and more. Hit the beats and notes, follow the ORDER that the structure is based in and start winning more deals.

Where do they want to be? Goals/future

We start off by telling them where they could be. What is their goal? What are their desires and what future do they want to see? I believe that we are goal-oriented animals and we move towards goals and we want to see those goals (or dreams) come to fruition.

Fantasies, goals, dreams, ambitions, futures, desires, needs, wants. What are the top 3 things that your customer wants? Boil that down and identify the absolute topmost powerful "I'll crawl over broken glass to get it" goal.

In the Benefit bucket/sales ammunition section of Chapter 3: Benefits And Futures, we looked at structuring bullet points in a way that clearly identified how to position a benefit or desire. In Chapter 2: From Products To Offer, we looked at the desired future that your customers have. Those parts are what you want to use here, in this section of the sales letter.

Webpage/sales page/optin page

Use a compelling headline and make it extremely clear that the rest of this page is focused on helping the reader achieve this goal.

Sales letter

Longer sales copy, either printed or online, would use a strong headline like above, but then also spend a paragraph or two telling the story of the beautiful future that someone could have if they followed this process. Testimonials, case studies, screenshots and results work well here. Mix up sales copy with proof.

Webinar

For a classic sales webinar, start off by outlining the goal that you're going to help them achieve, then spend a couple of slides again with testimonials, proof and screenshots. And include more detail about what they'll walk away with or be able to do/have/see/feel, if they watch the whole training.

When you transition from the opening section of the webinar, into the sales close part of the webinar, repeat the goals and position the offer for people who "are serious about [goal]".

Sales pitch

Either extremely short (i.e. elevator) or longer pitches, start with a strong desirable future that the listener would be interested in. It could even be posed as a question. "How would you feel if you could retire at 40, still have a fantastic income AND pay off your mortgage?"

Proposal

In a written proposal, either short or longer and more formal, start off with a clear statement about what the proposal will help them get and have a few bullet points about the goals which they have stated to you. The closer to using their language, the better.

Where are they now? Problem/escape

Now we need to agitate the problem and show them just how good that future can be, by looking at the problems they're facing now. This is what they need to escape, fix or change. This is where they are now. In chapter 2 we looked at what their life is like before working with you, this is where

234

you want to use it.

Make sure to spend as much, if not more time, on the problems aspect of your messaging. We are goal orientated animals and as a rule, we tend to move towards goals. However, our defences usually come up after the initial piqued interest of hearing a desirable goal. We need to agitate the problems that the reader/listener is facing. There is a phenomenon called The Trough Of Despair. It's a psychological phenomenon whereby people are so compelled by a goal that they start changing their life or undertake a new task, in order to reach that goal. The goal is the desired future, better life and what they want. However, after a while, people start to think that it's really not worth the effort. They'll start to cut back, slow down or stop. The apparent investment isn't worth the payoff.

Identifying and agitating their problems is a good way to remind them just how bad things are. If the frisbee is the goal for my dog, teasing her and waving it around is agitating it and REALLY makes her want to chase it.

Webpage/sales page/optin page

On your webpage, the problem section is where you can use a bullet point to really drive the point home. Use a bullet point like "No more sleepless nights! How to get a great nights sleep (even if you have to wake up early)" or "Eliminate late payments and never have to chase a customer again".

Sales letter

For longer sales letters or webpages, you can spend a few paragraphs telling a story (think of it as a tragedy) to your reader, about the soul crushing problem you or someone else experienced. Talk about their frustrations, stresses, worries, fears and roadblocks. This is the part of the story your audience will identify with the most. Use bullet points as sub-headings and expand on the tragedy of the problem – really agitate it.

Webinar

During webinars I like to tell a story of the same problem that I faced or a case study of someone who had the same problem. I don't go into how they solved the problem yet, I really dig into the dramatic, painful experience that I/someone had and how it affected their life. This is essentially the sob story and misery section of the webinar and it's critical that you lay it on thick.

Sales pitch

People love hearing their problems and how their life is harder than others. During a sales pitch, if I'm speaking to the customer, I'll tell them their story of their problems and how hard it is to deal with their situation. More than anything, the angle here is sympathy and understanding. No matter what the problem is, I clearly demonstrate that I'm on their side, I understand their situation and remind them how difficult it is.

Proposal

In my proposals, I'll bullet point the problems and quickly reiterate the problems. Focusing on the top 5 problems that they're facing, I won't go into too much detail as the "sale" has already been made in the customer's mind, but it doesn't hurt to reinforce and remind them.

What happens if they stay there? Trend/consequence

Often ignored in sales copy and web pages, the consequence section of your copy and story can often be what pushes customers to make the change. It's sad to say that most overweight people can deal with heart failure and even death, but that isn't the consequence. The consequence might be that their grandkids grow up without them. The consequence is essentially "here's what happens to your greatest fears and goals if you don't take action today".

Webpage/sales page/optin page

On an optin page or web page, I'll use the consequence in a bullet point such as "the only method to avoid sudden taxes" or "How I changed my diet to see my grandkids grow up". Or, I'll use it as a sub-heading in the title, under the main heading with something like "Never have to worry about money or sales again".

Sales letter

In a sales letter, I'd not only use a sub-heading like the above examples, but I'd also explain a little more in a further paragraph. Under the section where I write about their problems, I'd go into more detail about what could happen if they don't take action today. Sometimes I call this a knife-twist. Really digging the problem home and exacerbating their worst fears. Finally, I'll use the consequence as a close later to get them to act today. Consequences make for brilliant urgency closes.

Webinar

During the webinar, I'll spend a slide or two talking about the consequences of not taking action. But the power of the webinar is making the sale there and then, which is why I tend to agitate the consequences more during the close and calls to action. "Do you worry about...?", "Are you prepared to..." and "If you're fine with..." are great starters to use to frame the close.

Sales pitch

During a sales pitch, I'll focus on the consequences as much as the problem and again use it to drive the point home. Then, during the close, I'll use it to answer any objections and remind them of the call to action. For example, if someone says "I'm not sure this is the right time" I'll return with "I agree, you should have done this sooner really (reframing their timeline) and if we don't start today, you'll have to deal with larger tax bills in future. So we can start working to prevent that today, we just need a signature and a deposit".

Proposal

In the proposal stage, I like to include one quote in large type-face font to finish the problems section. "If [customer] doesn't develop a new marketing strategy today, they'll be forced to compete harder with rising competition in a matter of months".

What mistake do most people make trying themselves/ what have they tried before?

We have an anchoring problem as human beings where, if we've tried something before we tend to have a problem believing that something else could work if our method didn't. "But I've tried dieting before! It doesn't work!" When they're reading your copy or listening to your message, if they're interested in the problem you're solving, their natural defences will come up and say "I've tried this before" and you need to address that.

Webpage/sales page/optin page

The easiest way to address the mistake in the past, is with a simple brackets/parentheses at the end of the headline. I.e. (even if you've tried every diet on the planet) or (even if your Facebook ads haven't worked before). You can also use this as a bullet point on the page, framing it as a question such as "why beginners always fail with email marketing because they INSIST on using autoresponders".

Sales letter

In a sales letter, I like to add the brackets to the end of my headline just like the webpage. Setting the scene for the rest of the letter. However I also like to elaborate on the mistakes that people make, in the letter itself, fleshing out the story that the reader would have experienced themselves. Typically I'll put this in the letter after the problems and consequences section. It's a bit like a movie. Our hero is given a quest (promise) and needs to overcome a hurdle or enemy (problem). If they don't face the challenge head on and conquer it, they'll face certain doom (consequences) and usually there is a tale of foreboding or warning that someone else has tried to solve this problem in the past and failed (mistake). Or, they themselves have tried before and failed. Think about some of your favourite films, books and TV shows and stories. It isn't the "problem" or enemy that's compelling, it's the hero overcoming their own failures or rectifying the failures of those before them. Redemption is the most powerful human desire of them all. Conquering yourself and your own failures is what most people strive to achieve. As Edmund Hillary put it, we don't conquer the mountain, but ourselves. Don't skip the mistake section of the sales letter, it's probably the most powerful piece of the whole letter.

Webinar

Similar to the sales letter, I like to put a couple of slides in talking through the mistakes that I have made myself and that I see others make. Examples, screenshots and case studies work very well here. I like to also explain why their previous attempts failed AND (most importantly) explain that it ISN'T their fault. They were either lied to, coerced or something else that removes blame. That means I can move past the objection without it feeling like I'm attacking the viewer.

Sales pitch

During a sales pitch, I'll focus on what the client has done before and why it needs to change. Rather than branding it a "mistake", I'll explain why it no longer works or what needs to be done differently now. Combining this with the consequences section can be particularly powerful. For example:

If ABC Mining doesn't address these problems, they'll find their share prices slowly creeping down until critical mass and a sudden plummet in stock price (consequence). Previously, we've focused on large strategic partnerships with suppliers and manufacturers, however that isn't as powerful any more because of the public image of those companies also. So instead, we need to focus on internal key people of influence and promoting them as ambassadors, rather than relying on outdated external partnerships (mistake).

Proposal

The proposal is similar to the sales pitch, but I'll address the mistakes made as a couple of bullet points or even a single sentence or quote. Summarising the core of the previous activities that haven't worked or no longer work, I'll use it to set up the following sections.

What belief/myth do they have about getting there?

"Everyone knows that..." and then following that statement there is a torrent of nonsense that isn't true. Or at least, doesn't have to be the only truth. At some point, during reading your content or listening to you, people's internal defences will come up and object to whatever you're telling them. Similar to mistakes, these are reasons that they shouldn't listen to you. So you need to address them face on.

Webpage/sales page/optin page

On a webpage I like to sometimes swap out the mistake that I put in the brackets, at the end of a headline, and use a myth or misconception instead. Usually with the structure "even if...". For example, "The 5 fastest weight loss methods on the planet (even if you don't want to diet)." Or, "Here's how to buy a buy-to-let property (and no, you don't need a huge deposit). We address the myth or misconception in the headline.

I might also use the myth as a bullet point on the page, countering any objections the reader has. For example: Why you DON'T need expensive cameras to start filming YouTube

242

content. Addressing the myth that the reader has in their mind head on. All we're trying to do, is remove friction and excuses.

Sales letter

Sales letters will also need to spend a paragraph or two on myths and mistaken beliefs that people have about the solution. If we think of any action that you want the reader to take, they have internal and external roadblocks or excuses. Reasons for them NOT to take action. Internal ones are mistakes that they've made or their own self-limiting beliefs (more on that next). External excuses are things like myths that are outside of their control. In a sales letter, I'll bring up the myth and explain why it's wrong and why they needn't worry about it.

Webinar

During a webinar, I use the external roadblock of the myth, during the closing section of the talk. Webinars need to get to the point and while aggravating the problem is great with things like the mistakes and problems section. I like to address the myth or misconception during the close, when they're close to buying. I'll make an offer, tell them the call to action and spend a slide or two addressing the myth to remove the objection after that, treating it as a close. "Of course everyone knows that you need to hire expensive consultants (myth), but I know that's just not true. With our training, your team become their own consultants at half the price. And you can get started today by...(CTA)"

Sales pitch

Myths and misconceptions do really well in sales pitches, either right at the start or at the end. Don't use them in both places, but what I DO like to do is to use a case study of someone who believed the myth and why they were wrong. I'll even try to do a comparison where someone chooses option A (our product) over option B (the myth) and what happens.

Proposal

I'll use a myth in a proposal as a bullet point or in the opening paragraph. I don't spend too much time going over the myths in a proposal as the customer has already decided to buy and should be over these types of objections before they close.

What self-limiting beliefs are preventing them from taking action?

"Things" don't stop people from taking action. Thoughts, are what stop people from taking action. You as a salesperson could lay out the most comprehensive, structured, easy-to-follow and evidence-based plan to your customer, and STILL have resistance because...some bullshit excuse. Self-limiting beliefs will kill your sales faster than any other objection and they need to be addressed.

Webpage/sales page/optin page

On a web page that's short, I'll call the self-limiting belief out in the bullet point or the "even if..." suffix that I might add onto the heading e.g. How to stop biting your nails (even if you think you can't do it). Or I'll use it in a bullet point and rewrite it as a benefit e.g. *How my fear of losing money made me smarter at investing or Why you HAVEN'T saturated your email list yet even if you think you have.*

Sales letter

During a sales letter, I'll confront self-limiting beliefs after the trend or myth section. Spending a paragraph or two talking about the reason that most people don't take action. This is a brilliant place to put a real-life story or case study to demonstrate how someone changed their life and made a decision to make their life better.

Webinar

During webinars, I like to use limiting beliefs as a slide towards the start of the content, and as a close. I'll repeat the same limiting belief, or group of beliefs for both the beginning and end slides, pushing that the product helps eliminate or overcome those beliefs and how we can help.

Sales pitch

During a sales pitch, I'll frame the self-limiting belief as an objection or complaint that other customers have had, and how we addressed it or eliminated it. For example, when we pitched a large telco company back in 2016, our price was WAY over what others were offering. And typically, corpo buyers' self-limiting beliefs are around making the wrong decision or worrying that they'll have to clean up after us all the time. The solution was simple, a quote from a previous customer saying "Mike and his team listened to us and we never felt that we had to chase or clean up after them. It was the smartest decision we made for our marketing department."

Proposal

During the proposal stage, I tend to ease off the self-limiting beliefs until/unless there is a strong objection during the closing stage. If a customer doesn't want to buy there and then, I'll dig into the close and find out what's stopping them. Usually, by this point, it's a self-limiting belief. So I'll make sure I have an idea of what those could be before I turn them.

What are the steps to the method?

How do you eat an elephant? One bite at a time. I'm staggered at how many proposals and pitches I see where the salesperson never even explains HOW the customer is supposed to solve their problem. Explain the steps to the method (not in deep detail – you'll just bore them) and remind them throughout this section that YOU can help do this with/for them.

A quick note on "explaining the method": Lots of businesses are afraid of explaining the methodology of their

246

process to the customer, lest the customer disappear and steal their ideas and just do it themselves. First, your process is probably not so unique that no one else has ever thought of it. Besides, people like to hire people with a plan. They don't want to do it themselves. They want you to do it and them to get the glory. Secondly, in Spring 2021 I was diagnosed with cancer and a ruptured kidney. I had a Urologist explain the procedures to me including four rounds of surgery and chemotherapy. The method explained to me made me feel a part of the process. I didn't thank him and his team for his time, leave the hospital and buy a scalpel to try and do it myself.

Webpage/sales page/optin page

On a simple optin page I'll just explain the number of steps and what the "steps" are i.e. hacks, stages, ideas, principles. E.g. 3 killer investment hacks that anyone can use to save money.

Sales letter

For the sales letter, I'll list out in bullet points the stages of the process, spending about 1/4 of the letter on the method. I don't go into explicit detail, but I make sure to introduce the method, give it a name, explain the benefits of the stages and end the section with a summary. For example: That's why we have the 6A Framework. Audience, Amount, Assets, Authority, Attention, Action.

Sell Futures, Not Features

▢ *Define the perfect niche that LOVES to buy from you with Audience discovery*

Remember, only Sell Your Service uses the 6A Framework to get your business the five figure sales it deserves.

You know how to write benefits. Don't turn the sales letter into an instruction manual. Look at infomercials and see how they turn steps of a process or product into a clear and desirable benefit. List the benefits, not the stages. Sell futures, not features.

Webinar

Another mistake people make with webinars and sales letters, is spending too long on the methodology section. It's a trap – don't fall for it! All you'll get is bored customers, even if they think they want to know it all. What's the #1 rule for engaging content? Always leave them wanting more! If they have questions about how it works, or more detail, respond with "I'd be delighted to share more details with how it works, in depth, with examples. What's your number and I'll book a call for one of our team to go over your plan with our method". With webinars, just like the sales letter, I'll go over the method, but we do it twice. The first time is the shorter, edited version or one small part of the wider process. That's the content of the actual webinar. The second time is the wider view of the whole process or method, but during the sales stage after I've delivered the content part of the webinar.

It's a simple idea and don't overthink it. Invite people to a webinar explaining how to solve one small and specific problem. Then if they want more help, or if they want more results, then explain that you've got a wider solution that can help them further, faster and easier.

Sales pitch

I basically use the sales letter framework during my sales pitch. After going over the promise, problems, myths and trends, I'll introduce the solution, go over the bullet points and stages, and then summarize the method at the end. I'll also remind them that WE can help them with this method.

Proposal

The method is split into 3 sections during the proposal.

- ☐ Solution
- ☐ Investment
- ☐ Timescale

Explain the solution with bullet point benefits. Give them an idea of cost (don't get too detailed, high level is fine) and tell them how long it'll take. Each section only needs to take half a page each.

What's the next step (close)?

Without question, the most important part of any sales copy or pitch or message – tell them how to buy from you. If I ever see another proposal, sales page, pitch, webinar or presentation or advert that forgets to tell me how to give my money, it'll be too soon.

Webpage/sales page/optin page

ENTER YOUR NAME AND EMAIL ADDRESS TO GET FREE ACCESS!

Just enter your name and email and I'll send you access right away.

Do you think it's obvious what someone should do next? It's not. Make it more obvious, more clear and more specific. Tell them what they need to do. Rule #3 of selling: Make it easy for the customer to give you money.

Sales letter

One of my favourite video genres on YouTube (and there are a lot of these) is people prematurely celebrating a win. Running, cycling, swimming, motorbike racing, formula 1. There are dozens of examples where someone comes down the final straight and throws their arms up in celebration. Then at the final second, the person behind them passes them and claims first place, because they knew the golden immovable rule of winning. It ain't over 'til it's over. You MUST cross the line. Your customers and readers MUST be told explicitly what to do next and right now in order to win. They need clear, simple and easy to follow instructions.

- ⊠ Sign this digital document
- ⊠ Send over the deposit

It's almost certainly not more complicated than that. Hell,

Sell Futures, Not Features

it might be "click here and enter your card details". Do NOT take for granted that they know that they must cross the finish line. YOU are the coach, screaming at the runner to cross the line and the customer is the runner, celebrating early. GET. THEM. OVER. THE. LINE.

Webinar

Same story – I'll repeat the call to action between 5 and 10 times on the call. Each time with a slide, a link and what they need to do. After each slide, I'll go over a close or a reason why they should buy, and then I'll repeat the CTA slide. I want their great-great-great-great-grandchildren, in 200 years, to know what the call to action is. "Grandpa? Did you go to sellfuturesnotfeatures.com to order?"

"Why yes little Jimmy 3000, I did."

Sales pitch

The weakest weak milksop watered down pitches in the world end with "any questions?" It's like finishing sex with a survey on "was it good for you?" Your sales pitch should absolutely, categorically end with the exact steps the customer needs to take. "And we can get started today. We just need a signature here and a deposit. Sign here."

"Woah woah woah, slow down," the customer says "let's think this over. I have a few questions." Awesome – I'm glad you've got questions, but you KNOW what the final step is. I know you've got questions, but it's more important that you know how to buy.

Proposal

During the proposal I will put the actual "sign here" button or line on the contract. It's the first part I'll write of the whole proposal. It comes at the end of the proposal and I'll repeat what the CTA is after each objection, just like with the sales pitch and webinar.

Remember, these kinds of templates are more impactful when written down. Make sure to download our entire 9 part roadmap to help you sell futures, not features for free at sellfuturesnotfeatures.com/workbook.

Sales calls

Sales messages and letters are extremely useful. They do a huge amount of the heavy lifting and if you had a webpage, optin page, sales letter, webinar, pitch and proposal for your product, you'd be lightyears ahead of your competition. As a rule, I like to have as many supporting pieces of sales collateral as possible for my products.

However. That does NOT mean you can't sell something until you've got those pieces. Sales calls i.e. getting on a phone, Zoom, Skype or even in person is still THE most effective sales method that I know of. The "Paid discovery/deep dive" method outlined in chapter 4 is probably my favourite sales method above all else. Running live sales calls is a very similar process and can work wonders.

Sell Futures, Not Features

Don't think that you can't sell just because you don't have the materials above. Many people in this book are going to over-think or overcomplicate this process. Should I have a qualification call, then a sales call, then a paid discovery call? Should I offer a paid growth session before I sell a larger project to them?

There are two immovable laws of selling:

1. Make it easy for the customer to give you money

2. You can't reach an agreement if one of you disagrees

Other than that, there IS no perfect method. Some of you will use a series of social media posts, chats and a couple of calls. Some of you will have 3 calls, a longer pitch and a proposal. Don't believe ANYONE who tells you that their method works better than anything WITHOUT testing it. You are going to have to test what works for you, your product, your market and your sales process.

Are their methods that make life easier? Of course. Are their methods that will probably work? Of course. But don't over think it. If you WANT a process that I believe works and I've used to sell everything from car rentals, to software, consulting, coaching and video games, use the below.

1. Build some kind of audience that you can start having conversations with

2. Ask them via email, social, calls etc. if they're interested in solving [problem] or achieving [result]?

3. If they are, either immediately call them or text or message them via social

4. Ask them some easy qualifiers

    a. What kind of X are you?

    b. What's your biggest problem?

    c. I saw you were interested in my post/email about X, why is that?

5. Then offer them a quick 1:1 10 minute call

    a. No pitch, no sales

    b. Just see if we can uncover their top 3 problems

6. Remind them of the time and date

    a. Our software retainerbreaker.com can book appointments and remind people

7. Run the call and ask your qualification questions

8. Don't answer questions

    a. But if they have questions, offer to answer them on another longer call

9. On the call, if they're qualified and you think you could sell to them, offer a longer 45 minute call

    a. If they're not suitable, tell them and let them know you'll be in touch with something more suitable later

10. Run a sales call similar to the paid discovery call for FREE where you just uncover lots and lots of

problems

11. Dig deep into their motivations and frustrations

12. Every problem that comes up that YOU can solve, ask them "if we had a way to solve [problem] would that be worth talking about?

13. When you have a list of their problems you can solve, ask them if they'd like to hear how you can help

14. Break your pitch up into small, easy to understand chunks of the process

    a. Keep it high level, light and less "process" and more "model" i.e. rather than telling them how you'll build them an email marketing campaign to re-engage old subscribers, tell them "if we got previous contacts to become interested again and buy from you, does that sound like it could be a good idea? Because we can do that with our Engage Plan."

15. When you've made your pitch, ask them "where would you like to go from here".

16. They'll ask the price and the terms

17. Tell them the price in one sentence, make it clear and don't talk around it

    a. It's eleven hundred dollars

18. When they ask what's next, start to close them

Sell Futures, Not Features

19. If you can't close them on a call, give them a written offer of some kind, book in another call and close them later/follow up

This is just a high-level overview. It's basically, get people on a call to qualify them, get them on a second call to sell to them and so on. You could sell a discovery call to them. A deeper audit or interview. And then use THAT to sell an even bigger product. What you're doing on each call is getting them to give you ideas on what they'll buy. Keep stacking that up and you'll reach larger and larger sales.

Summary:

- ☐ Sales is a game of consistency. Following a pattern or script is going to yield greater results than just winging it each time

- ☐ Whether it's 1:1 or to a mass audience of millions, sales messages follow the same story beats. Don't overcomplicate the story just because it seems familiar. People like familiar

- ☐ Repetition is key. Repeating the same framework for your particular audience and sales media AND repeating the problems and goals. Don't assume that just because you've said something once to one person, that it's really sunk in

- ☐ End all your sales calls, conversations and content with a call to action. I cannot stress this enough.

Sell Futures, Not Features

Write that FIRST so you don't forget

Chapter 7 - Closing the deal

Closing the deal is responsible for 100% of the revenue that your company makes. "Close but no cigar" doesn't cut it. The cold hard reality is that if you don't close the deal, you don't get paid. You could spend (and this happens more than you might think) thousands or even millions of dollars on a sale, only to fall at the last hurdle.

You can't pay your overheads, staff and bills with "almost". Either you get the deal, or you don't. In this chapter we're going to talk about closing the deal, the close. This is where we make the exchange and get the money from the customer, confirm the sale and start working with them.

The sell-objection-buy diagram

One of the most common mistakes that people make when selling, is thinking that the sale is made if and when there are no objections. An objection, is something the customer says or does which prevents them from buying. We'll talk about types of objections later (price NOT being one of them), but safe to say that there are hundreds of reasons that someone might not buy from you. The key is making sure that you allow them the space to tell you their objections. The misconception is that with enough sales, there are no objections. And in fact it's exactly the opposite, you absolutely need objections before you make a sale. The objection comes before the sale.

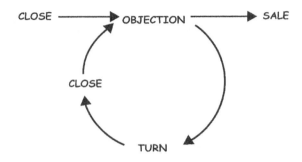

Figure 12: Sell - Objection - Close - Buy

In order to get the most from this model, let's be specific about the language and definitions we're using.

Close: the close is both an event and an action. "The close" is the call to action you give to the customer i.e. sign here. However, close or closed is also the state that the deal or customer is in, for example, Mike closed the deal with XYZ Corp. Another term for the state of the close, would be "sale". I.e. we made the sale with ABC or we closed the sale with ABC.

Objection: an objection is an expression or feeling of discontent with the next steps. It prevents people from taking the next step and closing. Timescales, trust, needs, money, risk. These are all reasons that people give in order to prevent buying and prevent closing.

Turn: the turn is how you listen to the objection and work through the objection with the customer. This is when their fears are laid to rest and they accept the answer and move on, either to buy (close/sale) or another objection.

Of you'd like some prompts or reminders, you can find them at sellfuturesnotfeatures.com/workbook.

We'll send you the worksheets that accompany this book for free, straight to your email. Plus, you can follow the exercises along in this book and be one of the action takers.

The close comes before the objection

Most people believe that their job is to do so well at sales, that they don't need to answer any objections. It's as if they believe that their pitch or sales letter is so compelling, that the customer won't have any objections. This is cancer to your close rate. It'll kill your revenue if you continue looking for that path.

Others believe that the route to a close or a sale, is to sell sell sell, then hear the objections, then close. In their mind they believe that they'll give a load of reasons to buy (selling), then the customer will give a reason not to buy (objection) and then when they've answered that, they'll close.

Both of these are wrong because it puts the order of events in the wrong order. What should happen, and what really happens is you sell, then you close, the customer gives an objection, and then you close again. The objection is part of the close. It's the other half of the agreement. The close doesn't happen without the objection, and if it does it's either rare or (more likely) dangerous.

After your pitch, presentation or sales letter, you offer a call to action to the customer. Sign here, click to buy, send a deposit. That's how you should end ALL sales calls and messages. You are saying to the customer "I've done all this work to help you and here's how we can help each other – take this step." What you are risking of course, is rejection. Good.

You want to be rejected at this point. You want the customer to object. You want to hear their objections because until this point, they haven't had to put anything on the line. You haven't asked them to put their money where their mouth is. It's the difference between asking your mates if your business idea is a good one (of course they'll all say yes) and asking them if they'll buy. This is the part where they put skin in the game and they step up to their end of the bargain. You're forcing their hand and they need to make a decision. You are calling their bluff and you want to hear what they have to say. And they will have something to say (or do or feel).

Most people are anxious when they ask for the sale. They get a little nervous and start to talk around the close. "Well, um, how did you find the presentation? Do you have any questions?" It's as if they want to avoid hearing objections because they're worried they'll lose the deal. Lots of salespeople don't offer the close because they're worried about hearing the objection, thinking that'll make them less likely to make the sale.

The exact opposite is true. You want to hear the objection as fast and as clearly as possible. I purposefully offer the close earlier than most people would be comfortable with, because I want to hear the objection. In fact, I'm excited to hear the objection because to me, an objection is a REASON to buy. When a customer says "um...well..." and then gives a reason they can't buy right now, what I hear is "Mike, help me understand why I should buy this right now."

What the customer is saying, when they give an objection, is "I want you to show me how I can justify this purchase even though...[objection]". When you start to hear objections, what you're hearing is the customer trying to find excuses to buy. They're not giving reasons to quit, they've looking for reasons to start. Internally, they're asking you to help them. But because humans are a funny bunch, they only think that internally. They would never dream of saying "Mike I love this but help me justify this cost to my manager." Why? Because they want to appear (both to you and themselves) in control.

Saying NO is the control move. The person who says no,

is the one in control. No is the ultimate expression of control and is only used by the person who is in control of the situation. Yes is a term of submission, no is a term of power. It's harder to say no and no returns control to the person who can say it. Ever heard the term "the only person who wins a negotiation is the person who can walk away"? That is saying that the only person who wins a negotiation is the person who can say no.

Do you want fries with that? No

Do	you	want	to	make	that	a	large?	No.
Do	you	want	to	go	out	with	me?	No.
Do	you	want	to	buy		this?		No.

Do you want to jump off a cliff? No.

The person who says no is the one who has the power. So, in the customer's mind, THEY need to appear in control and give you a NO or several "Nos" in order to appear in control. In their mind, they see a yes as submission. Even if they're buying something they need and want, they still see that purchase as a yield. Ever seen someone hesitate over buying something that would genuinely make their life easier or better or safer? It's because saying "yes" yields control over to something or someone else. It might be a complete nonsense made up internal submission, but it is a submission in their eyes none the less.

And here's the funny thing, the close IS a negotiation. But

not the type you're thinking of. Most people see sales vs. customer relationship as a push-pull dynamic. Making the sale is a "win" and shows that they somehow beat the customer. Many customers worry that the salesperson is trying to do just that – win. With them somehow on the other side of the table. Like it's a game and you're trying to outsmart the customer to make a sale. Many salespeople believe that if they're clever enough and quick enough, they can perform mental gymnastics on a customer to get them to sign. They never saw it coming. This is the thinking of a moron. It's mistaking brute force for strategy. The route to sales and selling, is seeing the close as a negotiation where you're BOTH on the same side.

If the customer didn't want it, they'd just say "I don't want it". The world's best marketing, adverts, social media campaigns, cutting edge features, influencers, peer pressure and sales tactics can't make me want something that I don't want. Many people have and want an iPhone. You could spend billions on targeting just me and trying to sell me one, but the cold hard truth is – I don't want one. When a customer gives an objection, they're telling you that they DO want to buy. But that they need help justifying the cost and investment and energy of taking action.

The close i.e. the offer of the exchange, needs to come first. You need to put your cards on the table and make the offer first before the customer has a chance to "reject" you.

Remember though, you're looking for that rejection because it means you're uncovering why they will or won't buy. If you're ever at the stage of the close, you must remember that you wouldn't be here if there wasn't something they're interested in. Now we're just ironing out the details.

Some people are easy sales - 2%

I'll be sure to give a list of my favourite closes and objection handles later, because sometimes the simplest questions work. Roughly speaking, every time you ask a customer "so would you like to buy?" 2% of them will say yes. They might have an objection that's easy to answer or ask for some clarification around some of the terms. But overall, they're an easy sell and they buy straight away. Because these sales go smoothly, people believe that this is the type of sale you should be looking for. Unfortunately, the saying "success has defeated you" applies here, because if you land one of these easy sales, you'll look for them everywhere and assume that this is how all sales should go. Therefor if a longer or more resistive sale comes in, you'll drop it because you believe that all sales should be simple and easy. Take these as an easy win, but understand that you could be missing out on 40x – 50x more sales with a little more time and persistence.

Some are sales soon - 2%

The next set of "easy" sales come soon, but not immediately. These are people who are ready to buy in the next 90 or so days. They might even check back in with you after that time, to see if the deal is still available. Again, take these as an easy win and focus on the other 96%.

Most need more closing - 96%

You are almost certainly missing out on 96% of sales, because they look a bit like hard work.

"When opportunity knocks, don't be surprised if it looks like hard work."

Unknown

When I talk to salespeople, they all tell me things like "I'm not afraid of hard work, I'll go all in and do everything I can to close the customer and get the deal." When I observe these same salespeople, what they really mean is "I'll give my pitch as I've learned it and be really excited but at the first sign of resistance or trouble, I'll assume they don't want to buy."

Hard work when it comes to sales isn't knocking on more doors or speaking in public. It's risking looking rude, foolish, stupid or all three. Hard work in sales is about knowing better than the customers and refusing to give up on them, even if they've given up on themselves. Eat your vegetables. Go for a walk. Take your medicine. You need to be the guiding light in your customer's life, even if they're straying.

When I look over a company's sales records, they almost always tell me "we need more leads". Their belief is that if they had more leads, they'd have more sales. In fact, the entire marketing agency industry is predicated on this belief. And as I have seen time and again, this belief is a total myth. Back in 2016 I worked with a software sales business. They sold the usual stuff from Microsoft products to cloud solutions and other productivity apps. The #1 complaint of the sales team was "none of our current leads want to buy" and again, we're talking about Microsoft and other massive multi-billion dollar software companies. Obviously they became so wealthy because no one wants to buy their products, right?

We built a lead generation campaign for them, and sure enough, the sales numbers were the exact same as before. So now, it was the new leads that didn't want the product. What are the odds?! A totally new set of customers and leads with the exact same problem as the last set! Talk about coincidence. I'm not a scientist, but the evidence was telling me that there were two things in common – the product, and the sales team. That year, Microsoft posted $85.3 billion in revenue [3], so taking a wild gamble, I thought it could possibly be the sales team. Upon further examination and after listening to their sales calls, I noticed three recurring factors in their lack of sales.

1. All successful closed sales were done within 15 minutes

2. All successful closed sales were made on the first or

---

[3]https://www.microsoft.com/investor/reports/ar16/index.ht

second attempt

3. The salespeople would drop the call after ONE objection

What this told me, is that the sales team were looking for the 2%. The easy sell. What they were doing is "dial and ditch" or "pitch and ditch". It looked a little like this.

"Hey Mrs. Customer, I'm calling from ABC and saw that you downloaded our Office 365 report. Is Office 365 something you're looking to buy?"

Either the lead said yes or no – easy sale. 2%.

If the lead gave any hesitation, objection, complaint, excuse or resistance, the sales person gave up. And some of the "resistance" wasn't even strong. We're talking things like, not picking up the phone. The call dropping because of bad signal. A question about the report or install time. This sales team had become so used to easy sales that they were ignoring massive potential in the market simply because they didn't want to push any further

Imagine what your sales numbers would be, if your current yearly sales goals were only 2% of the possible total. That turns a $100,000 business into a $5,000,000 business. All at the expense of a little fear and pride. You will surprise yourself if you refuse to give in a little longer. Make another call, close another objection, make another offer, follow up again and again and again. Build a relationship, be more curious, ask more questions and offer more solutions. That 96% of missed sales comes at the expense of risking being disliked a bit.

Imagine your job is to collect truffles in the forest. They can sell for between $1500 and $4000 per lb. Lets' say you manage to find 5lb, yielding around $20,000 in sales. What if I told you that there was another 250lbs in the forest, a little further in BUT you'd have to look stupid, people would call you rude and foolish. Wouldn't you go for it? That's another $980,000 in revenue. What if I also told you that the people who thought you looked stupid, occasionally bought from you AND many many more people would also buy. Doesn't this sound crazy?

That's what many salespeople and business owners are afraid of. They're afraid of following up more and worried that they might possibly be seen as rude, arrogant, annoying or persistent. When the reality is that they almost certainly won't be seen as or thought of as that. When you flip your mindset and start seeing the customer as on the same side of the table as you, you're not worried about looking stupid because it's a partnership. You're not worried about answering their objections and closing them again and again, because you've got bigger plans in mind.

The close is the exchange

In order to remove some of the emotional weight and fear

from closing, it's helpful to realise two things about closing, which can take the pressure off.

1. Selling is emotional, closing is logical
2. The close is the exchange

What this means is that the part where you say "do you want to buy?" and the customer responds with "yes please" is how you get the exchange started. The close is simply the exchange of one resource for another. It's the exchange of money, time, energy for something else. It's a purely logical and formatted process. It's funny because so many salespeople become emotional during the close, rather than the sale. Remember when we talked about how sales is a transference of enthusiasm? Well closing is an exercise in logic and methodology. When you as the salesperson start to become worried that you'll lose the deal, or emotional about the response from the customer, you're moving away from the logical part of the transaction.

Sell with emotion close with logic

Think about cashiers at a supermarket. You put all your goods on the conveyor belt. Billions of dollars in advertising for the store and the products you've chosen, plus the packaging, testimonials and experience have done the selling part. You have been sold on the products you've picked up. Now when you place those items on the belt, the cashier isn't thinking "oh no. I hope they want these. What if they don't really want to buy? What if they reject the offer?" They don't ask you "are you sure about these?" (unless you're buying 18 party-sized bags of Skittles after a particularly messy breakup – but that's another story). Cashiers are the world's greatest closers. They know that this is now the exchange. It's the logical part of the journey. The sale has been made and their job is to exchange goods for money. They don't go back to the sale. When you and the customer agree that their core need and want is X, and that's the best route forward, you move to the close. The customer is probably already sold. That's the funny part. In their mind, they've probably already made the decision to buy, so now your job is to iron out with them how they'll pay for it and how you'll deliver it.

Listen, agree, close

In the next chapter I'll give you my closes, plus common objections that I hear and how to handle them. I'll go over some specifics and templates, but as a rule, my "hack" for closing and objection handling has always been Listen, Agree, Close.

Lots of sales books talk about things like false closes and test closes. These are questions like "if we could do that for you, would that be of interest?" or "if that were the case would you be looking to buy?" It's kind of a way of testing to see if the customer is ready to buy. But in my opinion, salespeople rely on these too much and read into the answers.

Sell Futures, Not Features

The customer hasn't bought until the customer has bought. It's all too easy to listen to customers saying they're interested and they'll buy, until they turn around and say "well of course I didn't mean I'd buy today, I'd have to check with my husband/ wife/ bank manager/ clairvoyant." Don't overcomplicate the sales process with mind games, just listen, agree and close. And what does listening come after? Questions.

You will absolutely SMASH all your sales goals if you ask more questions. A few days ago while writing this chapter, I was called by a sales rep on the phone from a company that provides home workout equipment. It's one of those smart mirror things with a camera and a subscription plan. George would be horrified that an entire chapter from his book is now the sales pitch for a company like this. But I was interested either way. I had obviously given them my number at some point, and the rep clearly identified themselves as a sales rep. They immediately asked ME if I had any questions. We might think this is a smart way to get someone to talk, but it's not. At all. I asked something basic like "how does the 30 day challenge/refund work?" and he launched into a diatribe about the features, benefits, process and how it all works. They have two different models, classes, live classes, internet features etc. blah blah blah. He then said "I don't know if you've got kids but we offer loads of kids classes, only a few minutes in length…" and he spent a good 5 minutes talking about the kids classes. I don't have kids. Instead if he'd have started with questions like "do you have children" or "tell me about how you work out now" I'd have talked and talked and talked. YOU need to ask questions from the customer and then – LISTEN. Great salespeople are great listeners, not talkers.

You: So tell me Mike, do you have kids?

Me: No I don't

You: Well tell me about your home workout routine

Me: In workout every day, I guess I'm looking for a bit more structure. Plus, I recently had some pretty serious surgery so I'm having to recover from that.

If that salesperson had asked questions, listened and agreed (then closed) he probably would have made a sale. You need to be smarter than that. Ask questions, listen and AGREE.

Agreeing doesn't mean that you'll do whatever they say. Or that you even think they're right. It means that you're demonstrating that you can see it from their perspective. "Oh you don't have kids? Me neither" or "well then let's focus on you" or even just "OK, cool". Acknowledgement is as good as agreeing. It means you're not arguing against them. Ever wondered why having the last word in an argument is so important? Because the person who spoke last believes that they are right. Simply because no one else answered them. It's the reason your drunk uncle thinks he's so smart when telling people about his radical ideas, because people don't argue against him. He's taking silence as a sign of submission. When really, you're just ignoring him. When a customer gives an answer or an objection (as we'll see later) the most powerful thing you can do with them is agree with them.

You: Recent surgery huh? Yeah you'd need to be careful with that (agreeing) Can I ask what your biggest struggle with exercise is now? (question)

During the close, when you ask them to buy, it can seem harder to agree with an objection. It even sounds like a totally counter-productive method. But remember, you're on the SAME side as the customer. It's not a battle or a negotiation. It's working out if you can work together. It's seeing if it makes sense to work together.

You can't reach an agreement, if one side disagrees. It's pretty simple. It doesn't mean do whatever they tell you, nor does it mean that the customer is always right. It means agreeing with them and being on their side. Very broadly speaking, men (males) struggle with this more than women. I don't know why, maybe it has nothing to do with XX/XY chromosomes, but in my experience I have seen women approach the agreeable methodology much easier than men. Men tend to see things as right or wrong and want to beat the customer into submission. Women tend to be on the customers side and agree with them, even if the outcome is the same.

Again, totally based on anecdotes and personal experience. But think about when men and women are told about a problem or event. Men want to solve the problem or (and more infuriating) offer very useful hindsight advice on how they would have done it. Volcano eruption caused a flight delay? You should have bought travel insurance. Not the right size or shape? Yes it is – you're wrong. I have seen women on the other hand, approach problems with a sympathetic ear and agreeing with the customer, not offering them a solution, but being on the same side. Volcano disruption? How awful! That's very annoying. Not the right size or shape? Yes I agree, it's not perfect.

The customer wants to feel acknowledged and heard. They want to feel like their input matters. Remember, at this stage they're about to hand you a load of money. They're about to yield their trust to you and they want to know you've got their best interests at heart. Just try this the next time someone brings a problem to you. Don't offer to fix it or give them advice. Just LISTEN and agree with them. Let them be heard, not lectured. It takes practice, but eventually you'll agree with everyone and it makes life a whole lot easier.

Finally, we close them. It might be the first close or the hundredth. But you must end with a close. The close is the next step. The call to action. "If you sign here, and send the deposit, we can get started today" or "click here". Hear the objection, listen to the objection, agree, close.

Mike, I'm just not sure about the timing. It seems longer than we expected.

I agree, it's a fair amount of time. We can get started today with a signature and a deposit (listen, agree, close).
But what if we go over timescale and budget?

You're right to be concerned about that. We're extremely mindful of that also. I think your idea of weekly updates included in the project is a good idea. That's also our #1 concern. We can get started today with a deposit (listen, agree, close. Note how the turn of the objection – weekly updates – was credited as their good idea).

In the next chapter I'll give more closes, as ways to basically do the same thing. Show that you're listening, coming up with an agreement and closing.

The close doesn't benefit you, it benefits the customer

Here's how you need to think about closing. Closing the customer is the first time that they'll feel a benefit. It's the start of their life getting better. Can you remember booking a table or a holiday, or confirming a date for something, and feeling a sense of relief? That feeling that "at last! This is getting taken care of!" That feeling of relief is a benefit. It's one of the most compelling and desirable benefits you can provide. And closing the customer is the start of that benefit. In exactly the same way that you don't get paid until you close, the customer doesn't start to benefit until you close. And frankly, if your products and services are good, then YOU are giving them more than what they're giving you. Think about the concept of value. A customer buys because they feel that the price you're offering is worth less than the benefits and results. The benefits outweigh the price. So when you're closing someone, you could argue that you are losing out a little bit. You've decided to give them something in exchange for something of slightly less value. So therefor, the close benefits the customer more than you.

Earlier we did the "who benefits, who suffers?" exercise. During the close stage, right before I ask "do you want to buy? Sign here?" I imagine that list of people who will suffer if I don't make the sale. Me, my friends, my family, the customer, their friends and family, their customers etc. I visualise them being worse off if I don't close the customer there and then. That gets me over the line. I also visualise all the people who benefit when I close the customer. I'm just a fraction of the people who have any benefit from closing the customer. The customer benefits, their friends and family benefits, their customers, their staff, team, bank manager and so on. The close is the most exciting stage of the sales journey because it means you're about to make a difference. Just knowing that someone else (you) are taking care of these problems is enough for most people to feel happier. The exchange is confirmation of the desire. If someone wants to feel smarter or improve their status, or if they want to have better mornings or relationships, they don't get to start feeling that until they buy. They will start to feel that as soon as they hand over the money and sign the contract. The close doesn't just benefit you, it benefits the customer.

It's got nothing to do with price

"I want this for free. I want a discount. Can you give me more for less? I want it cheaper. This is too expensive."

"Haha, I agree! It's a lot of money. Sign here."

The trap that many salespeople fall into is believing that anything to do with price, money or payment is an objection. It isn't. Pricing is a problem.

When a customer says to you "that's too expensive", or "I can't afford that", did you know that's not an objection?

A lot of the time when customers are going through the closing process with us, and we say to the customer "okay this is going to be $25,000 or $100,000" or whatever the price is and they'll say "oh wow that's pretty expensive".

A lot of sales coaches are going to tell you that's an objection. It's not.

Saying it's too expensive or saying they can't afford the

product, or they don't have the money is not an objection. An objection is a reason why they don't trust you to deliver the results. When someone says "oh it's expensive" or "it seems like a lot of money" or "we can't afford that, we didn't expect it to be that much", I've often said in the past that that's your fault and that's still entirely true.

It's still your responsibility to understand what your customer's budget is. And a lot of the time when customers say "it seems really expensive. I don't know. If I can afford that. We don't really expect it to be that much. We don't have that much money in the account right now" etc. They're expecting you to come back and turn that objection.

99% of the time it's because they don't trust you, and there's an element of the buying process which you haven't clarified with them. You probably haven't gone out of your way to explain why this is the best deal in the universe, and that you're going to over-deliver compared to the amount of money that they're going to put in.

Here's what most sales coaches will teach you. They'll teach you that someone saying "that's expensive" or they can't afford that, is an objection and you need to turn that objection. The easiest way we know to turn an objection, are things like feel, felt, found.

"Hey I totally understand how you feel. A lot of customers felt the same way. But what we found is that the value we're going to deliver through this final project is going to outpace that $25,000 initial investment hundreds and hundreds of times".

Feel, felt, found.

But saying something is too expensive, is not an objection. Saying that they haven't got the money is not an objection. It's a problem.

The customer saying "this is expensive" is their problem. That's a framework in their state of mind, that they perceive your product as expensive compared to their situation.

It's not expensive, but customers are still going to say to you "wow this seems expensive. That's a lot of money" and the way that I get around that, is I agree with them. Then I tell them to sign and send a deposit.

When a customer says to me, "Well that's a lot of money. That's pretty expensive. I don't know if we've got that in the account right now." I'll reply with "I totally agree man it is expensive. What isn't nowadays? Sign this and send us a deposit."

That's the way that you want to start framing this particular problem. It's not an objection from your customers. An objection is when they say "okay but what if it takes longer than you say it will?"

Until they understand that process, that's an objection. That's a valid objection of something that you haven't covered. You could be the best salesperson in the world, deliver the most comprehensive in-depth value driven pitch ever, and the customer could still turn around to you and say "this doesn't seem like it's worth it. I don't know if we've got this kind of money".

That's their problem. Money is their problem. Their money is their problem. Their money isn't your problem. So if they come around to you and say that it seems very expensive or it seems like it's a lot of money, you agree with them.

Yes it is expensive. Yeah it is a lot of money. I don't doubt, that you don't have that in the account right now.
Sign here. Give us the deposit.

What they want to do is voice their opinions. It's kind of like that final resistance that kids use, before doing what their parents tell them to do. When you say "we've got to go put your shoes on, we're going to get in the car" and they kind of wait around. Teenagers are really good at this. They do everything they can to lengthen the process, where they still feel like they're in control. They feel like they need to give that final bit of resistance before succumbing to your level of control. That's what that problem is.

That's what the customer is saying when they say "this is pretty expensive." When a customer does say to you "wow this seems really expensive" a lot of sales coaches will teach you to do one of two things.

Sell Futures, Not Features

First turn the objection or secondly (and I've even seen some coaches do this) back down and negotiate down your price. Neither of those two are an option. Partly because it's not an objection. Someone saying that this is expensive or it's a lot of money or they don't know if they've got the money in their account right now – is not an objection. It's a problem and you solve problems in a very different way.

If someone said to you "oh I don't know if I've got the right kind of laptop to be able to view the pages" agree with them. That's a problem and it's something you'd be able to solve!

"Well actually you don't need a specific type of laptop because we're going to be building it. But also I can help you find the right kind of laptop. You don't even need something that's spectacular."

Or if the customer said "my iPad is so slow at loading pages. It won't even load the sales page." You say, "I agree. iPads suck don't they? Their speed is really really bad. Anyway, sign here, give us a deposit.

They're giving you a problem and they want you to solve that problem. This is not necessarily a case of them asking if you can reduce the price. That's a very different question.

First, customers will never say that. And the reason they won't say that, is because they don't want you to reduce the work that you're putting in. If a customer does say to you "this $25 000 it seems a little bit much, I was wondering if we could bring the price down a bit?"

Again, you can agree. The key to getting the deal or the key to getting an agreement – is to agree. Of course yes we can bring the price down. What elements of the delivery or the proposal do you want to get rid of? If you want to bring this down to $25,000, we can get rid of the sales page, and the sales email automation. We can get rid of all of that and you'll just be left with $20,000. How does that sound?

They won't want to do it. They'll say "we kind of wanted to keep all of it but pay less" and you go "ah I wish I could do that, but I can't. I know it's expensive. Sign here."

The difference is knowing when to sell and when to close. And when the customer tells you this seems a little bit expensive, I'm not sure if we can afford this – you agree with them. You say "I totally agree. What's not expensive in today's day and age, you know?"

"Everything seems to be running at a high premium price, especially premium products. Anyway, sign here. Send us over the deposit and we can get started today."

You're moving past turning the objection and you're helping them understand. You have a lot of people tell you that this is a big investment. You understand the level of trust and commitment that they're putting into this project. You're planning on putting in more than they are. You and your team are going to put in more, than the money they're putting in, because they're going to walk away with more than $25,000 worth of value.

But here's what a lot of people do. The mistake people make, is that when the customer says that it seems very expensive, they'll go back to selling. They'll go back to talking about the value you've got. They'll talk about amazing landing page sequences and how they're going to drive leads and they're going to drive sales. They'll talk about building out your sales automation process and obviously we've got consultation and design and blah blah blah blah blah.
None of that matters.

What you need to be working on, is agreeing with the customer. You need to say, "Yeah, I agree it is expensive. Sign here, send us over the deposit."

Some sales coaches will teach you to ask "how important is that to you?" when confronted with an objection.

If the customer replies with "Well it's pretty much the only important thing."

You've dug yourself into a hole that you're unable to get out of. Rather than trying to turn the objection or be clever or work around it or worse – go back to selling (which is the absolute last thing you should be doing), close the sale.

By the way, when you're at the sales stage and someone says to you "yeah this sounds great. Send us over the proposal." That's the closing stage. You don't sell anymore. That's the stage where you tell them to send over the deposit and sign here. Tell them we can get started on this today.

When a customer is saying to you, that they don't know and this seems a little bit expensive, don't go back to trying to sell them again. Because it's still going to be expensive when they get to the end. They're still going to be unsure if they've got the money. When you go back to that final closing stage, instead what you need to say to them is "yes I agree it is expensive. What isn't today right? Anyway sign here. Here's the deposit."

What you need to be doing is getting them over that line, and if they need to make up a story about how there's hardly any money in the bank, or they're not entirely sure, don't go back to asking questions. Don't say to them "oh...but you told me you had $25,000."

Don't worry about any of that. When someone says it's expensive, I agree with them and then say we can get started today. Here, sign here. Give us the deposit. I can even take a payment via credit card.

Frame it as being in a hurry to help your customers. You need to be in the position where you're saying to your customers that you know this is expensive. You're taking as much risk as they are. This is why you need to sign today and pay today, because I'm going to be able to fix whatever is broken in your business and we will take whatever is broken in your business and fix it.

I'm going to give you solutions and results. But going back over that is not going to change anything. Most customers are going to say "Wow that's fantastic. Thanks very much. Let's go ahead. That's brilliant." That's going to happen 99% of the time. Here's what's interesting, when you start making offers to customers, and you know you've got a bunch of people in your email list or in your address book. You start to think "I really should be emailing my customers and asking them 'do you want me to send over a proposal?'"

They're going to be fine with you taking control of the situation. It's a bit like dogs. They can smell fear, they can, smell hesitation, they can smell anxiety. But if you're confident you say "yeah, it is pretty expensive. But you know premium products are. Anyway sign here give me the deposit".

Most of the time people are willing to sign. If your price is crazy over and they say "WOW! We were expecting $10,000 not $25,000" then that's your fault, because you haven't qualified them enough. When a customer tells you that your product seems very expensive, that's not an objection. You don't need to turn it – you need to agree with them and then continue that closing process. Give them the deposit invoice. Give them the card machine or your PayPal details. And get them to sign a contract.

Assume the sale

What signals do people give that they want to buy from you? We're often told to look for buying signals and we might even do test or false closes to gauge how interested a customer is in buying. The problem is that these signals could be written in neon letters with fireworks and an audio-track saying "I want to buy" over and over, and salespeople still miss them. The miscommunication isn't down to the customer not giving buying signals, it's the salesperson not seeing or hearing them. I'll give you the strongest, most obvious and powerful buying signal in the world. One that if you can spot, will basically tell you that someone is absolutely interested in buying and they want to give you some money. Get ready to write this down and ask yourself "is the customer/lead doing [blank]?" because if they are, it means they want to buy from you. Get ready. The ultimate buying signal is:

The customer is talking to you.

If you are engaged with any kind of dialogue with someone, that is the strongest possible signal that they want to work with you. And from now on, anyone who engages with you, I want you to ATS. Assume The Sale.

Assuming the sale means assuming that the customer wants to buy. No matter their attitude, questions, objections, complaints, delays, excuses or mannerisms. Your job is to

287

assume that they want to buy. I have seen salespeople almost disbelieve that someone would want to buy from them, during the customer actively trying to hand over money. Have you ever had the situation where you want to buy and you're literally ready to get out your credit card, but the salesperson just won't GIVE you the product? It's called overselling and is a sign of a lack of confidence on behalf of the seller. If you've ever had someone continue to give you benefits and reasons to buy, almost arguing with you, even when you're ready to buy, that is overselling. As the customer, you presume that the salesperson knows what they're doing and they'll get around to closing and exchanging with you. But they don't know how to close and they're missing the buying signal.

As a salesperson, ATS is a method for pushing for the sale, without being pushy. It's knowing that in the back of your mind, you know that the customer wants to buy. They just have a little dance or routine that they need to go through, before they're willing to admit it to themselves.

One of my sales coaching customers sold ski and snowboard instructor packages. The company did a fantastic job of generating leads, but their sales team just weren't closing the deals. People were signing up for more information on HOW to become a ski/snowboard instructor. But for whatever reason, the salespeople had a hard time closing them and getting the deal. They brought me in for a little training and I asked the sales team "why do you feel you're not getting the sales from the people who want to become ski/snowboard instructors?"

- ☐ They say it's expensive
- ☐ They're not sure it's right for them
- ☐ They were just enquiring
- ☐ They'd have to get their parents' permission
- ☐ They weren't sure they were good enough

They had all these reasons and more, many of them similar to objections/excuses that you've heard yourself I'm sure. But to me, there isn't a good reason why someone wouldn't buy. Of course it's expensive, you probably are worried that you're not good enough or you need your parents' permission. But when has that stopped young people doing other stuff? I dug a little deeper and asked the salespeople "why aren't you still closing people even though they say these things?"

Because I'm worried about being seen as rude.

And there we go. That's the crux of the reason why the sales weren't being closed. The salespeople were worried that pushing past the objections or excuses or reasons, would make them seem rude or even like bad people. And it's a shame, because so many businesses struggle to make sales, purely because they're worried about looking rude. Which is why it's so important to assume the sale. Whenever you close the customer, or when they give you an answer or even a no, it's critical to assume the sale and believe that the customer wants to buy.

The internet and feel-good sales books are full of watered down and coward-based selling. Things like "how to sell without selling", "how to sell without being salesy" or "sales without being pushy". To me this is like saying you're really anti-war or anti-cancer. WHO is on the other side of that argument? Who is pro-war? What moron is pro-cancer? Who's giving training on "how to sell by selling" or "how to sell by being pushy?" What book is called "how to be more salesy"? It's middle of the road, watered down content sold to people who are naturally uncomfortable selling to other people. It's also massively dishonest. Because the people who are producing that kind of content think they're taking a stance on something. As if that gives them a radical and divisive viewpoint on a previously untouchable subject. It's a method of seeming like you have values and a niche and a unique perspective and even, a personality, when in fact it's just pandering to people's deepest fears and telling them "It's ok, you can lose weight and still eat all the ice cream and Oreos you want". Selling without selling, or whatever bullshit nonsense is being banded around by internet-feel-good gurus is like saying swimming without swimming. Or eating without eating. If you work in sales, or if you run a business, your job above all else (and this shouldn't be controversial) is to make money. Your absolute categoric priority should be – make money.

I see training seminars on "how to sell without sleazy sales tactics" which – by it's very definition, is a sales tactic. No one would ever proudly say they have sleazy sales tactics. No one says they're proud of their pressure based selling approach. The sleazy, slimy and disreputable aspects of selling are no different to the sleazy, slimy and disreputable methods of medicine, design, development, cooking, building houses, renovating a garden, sports, training, therapy, relationships and any other activity that humans are involved in.

Sales is no more or no less offensive than any other work or job. But, for some reason, people who work in sales are desperate to feel around the subject of "I don't want to offend people" and they want to be liked by everyone. I'm afraid to say that that is a human condition problem, not a problem of sales or selling. Your need to be liked and for others to have a good opinion of you is killing your sales chances. And the crazy thing, is that not selling to your customers, is more dangerous for your reputation, than trying to push the sale.

Yes, you should be pressuring your customers

Here's the undeniable but ugly truth. Something that is considered radical and divisive. You absolutely should be applying pressure to people who want to buy something. Pressure makes sales. It's unavoidable, 100% true and is the most moral thing you can do to someone buying a product.

Your customer wants to make a decision and take an action, because something inside them is driving them to do so. We talked earlier about people's day-to-day lives and what they're happy or unhappy with. People desire change, they desire better and they want more. If they're joining the gym or a diet program, it's because of a deep internal desire to do something different. It's because they want to BE different. If they're looking to change their servers or their car tyres, it's because of a driving force and a realisation within them that they need to do something different.

This is called pressure. If they don't make a change, or do something different, there are negative consequences. That's called pressure. If they need to be reminded that things still aren't good or where they want to be, that's called pressure.

- Losing weight so I can play with my kids and lead a longer life
- Start writing that book so I can leave a legacy
- Book a course to become a ski/snowboard instructor because I want to be one
- Moving abroad to be with my partner and start again
- Buy a video game so I can enjoy the story and action

All of these actions are the result of pressure. And guess

what? That pressure exists whether you're there to sell them a product or not. That pressure is a deeper internal drive that forces them to think about what could be bigger or different or better. The COST of relieving that pressure is BUYING. We are all being chased. Chased by time, entropy, mortality. The constant presence in the back of our minds is that one day, all of this goes away. THAT is pressure. Say what you want about salespeople, but the pressure they can apply is nothing compared to the inevitable calling of death.

So when the customer gives you an objection or an excuse, assume the sale. Assume that they want to buy BUT, they're afraid. The cost is there and it must be paid. There's nothing they or you can do about it. But know that they want to buy and they want to make the exchange. Assume that they want to buy because they're talking to you. What they're asking for, is a guiding hand through the process and for you to give them reasons TO buy. And what better reasons than the pressure they've given themselves? What better benefit than the ones that they're giving?

For my ski/snowboard course customer, I told the salespeople to ATS. Assume the sale. Assume that they're going to buy anyway. Even if they rant and rave and scream and shout (no – obviously that isn't going to happen and never does). But imagine the worst possible scenario and that they do end up buying. The fear is that you as the salesperson will try to sell over and over and end up with NO sale. That means you had to endure awkward questions and turning objections, only to end up with no sale. Instead, imagine that at the end of all that, the customer does want to buy. What would you be willing to put up with, or do, in order to get the sale? What if deep down, the customer is shy and too nervous to ask to buy. Incredibly, this is a huge problem with many sales. The customer isn't sure if they're good enough to buy. What if you're denying them an opportunity to make their life better, just because you're afraid of your feelings getting hurt?

When you talk to the customer, presumably you're asking them a lot of questions. What motivated you to buy? Tell me what you're interested in? Why now? Why are you looking at buying from us? Those are all reasons that the customer wants to buy, and if you're paying attention, somewhere in there is the internal pressure that they're facing to make a decision. If there was never any pressure from anywhere, no one would make any decisions or take any action. Everyone would just stay where they are. We NEED pressure to take action. Assuming the sale means asking those questions and then repeating back to the customer, after they give you an excuse or a reason not to buy "are you still looking to lose weight so you can play with your kids? Are you still interested in becoming a snowboard instructor, so you can board more and live in The Alps? Is it still important to you to change your servers so you're not spending so much time fixing them and you can start to leave the office at a respectable time?" Yes? Then let me take the deposit amount. What's the long card number?

You can quietly tip-toe around and decide that it's more important to be liked by other people (people who you're never going to meet again). Or you can take your customers by the hand and show them some real leadership. Help them make hard decisions and get over the price or cost and give them the benefits that they want. Presumably, you believe that your benefits are worth the cost. And therefor you should be proud to get them over the line. Remember that the close and sale doesn't benefit you – it benefits the customer. That's when their life starts to get better.

One last thing on assuming the sale. The more you believe in the back of your mind that when you ask a question and close a customer, that they want to buy, two things will start to happen.

1. You'll start to ask better questions, more frequently. You'll ask if people want to buy AND you will have more people say yes, more often.

2. You'll have more fun. You'll be more open and more relaxed, because you know people are going to buy. Therefor, more people will buy. There's nothing more attractive than confidence.

Sell Futures, Not Features

But Mike, what about those awful door-to-door salespeople like Kirby, who use huge amounts of pressure to make the sale. I don't want to be like them!

I once gave a talk and spoke about ATS and I talked about pressure. The lady asking this question stood up and spoke for about 5 minutes on her horror story. The MC had to eventually intervene and tell her to get to the point. In a nutshell, it was a story about how some Kirby vacuum people (or double glazed windows, or SKY TV, or charities etc.) gave her and millions of others the hard sell. So what do I think about that?

Well first of all, as someone who did used to sell like that, my first question is "why is that such a bad thing?" This threw her of course. She expected me to give a defence or an apology of some kind. But, what would be so bad about that? I asked her and she responded with another diatribe. "It's unethical, it's bad for my reputation and brand. I would be doing someone a disservice. I wouldn't want someone to think ill of me. I don't want to upset people and I certainly don't want them to think badly of me. I don't want them to buy a product they're not going to use."

This is a similar conversation I have with a lot of people. And here's the response I give. First, it sounds like you have a problem with your product more than anything. Do you believe that your product should absolutely be in the hands of at least every single person in your market? Maybe even the world? I do. I believe that my books and courses can benefit every human on the planet and I refuse to accept otherwise. I'll gladly sell into as many homes and businesses as I can, because I believe in my product. If you're worried about selling a product to someone who doesn't or can't use it, that sounds like a problem you've got with your marketing and qualification process. It sounds like you're not talking to the right people. Nothing to do with sales, closing or making money. That just sounds like you're worried people won't get anything from your product, which is a product problem.

As for the "brand" and what people think of you, you need to get over that. You have absolutely zero control over how someone else sees your business, your brand and you. I've got awful news for you. There are people who already don't like you. There are people out there who don't like you, because you refused to sell to them. There are people out there who don't like you even when they like your product and vice versa. Stop worrying about whether people will think badly of you. It doesn't matter.

One of the most confusing aspects of today's methods of communication, combined with the internet and the rise of social justice warriors, is everyone's feelings of superior morality. People love to tell you how eating meat is morally bankrupt. But then so is veganism. Drive a car? You might as well commit genocide. Only drive electric? You're killing the planet. Only drive fossil fuels? You're killing the planet also. Don't drive a car? You're either lazy or privileged. The internet has made it very easy for people to put together superior intellectual morality arguments and talk about how awful the extremes are, of their argument. So when I tell people to apply more pressure, work through objections and assume the sale, people love to jump into the extreme side of the argument and bring up poor sales practices from their real life or movies. But with all their superior intellect and ability to see more than everyone else, they forget the very simple concept of balance.

Life is about balance. Not extremes or taking sides or being A/B. It's about having a little balance. People don't like balance of course because it requires discipline, patience, thought, reflection, adjustment, meditation and control. People would rather stand on their side of the fence and give 100 reasons why the other end is absolutely deplorable and a blight on humankind. And the thing is, I agree. I agree that the other side is pretty reprehensible. But no one is asking you to go to the extremes, are they? I'm certainly not. A blanket statement like "pressure selling is disgraceful because [insert anecdote or isolated statistic]" is like saying "Enron committed fraud with US dollars, therefor all currency is used in fraud." Chill. Be cool. Seek balance.

If you're so morally upstanding and a paragon of deeper human issues, then use some of that big heart of yours and be a good example. Become the rule, not the exception. Show people how it can be done. Challenge yourself. Don't let other people's mistakes dictate how you act and behave.

Stay quiet

Give me the space to think and answer.

Something my wife told me, was that I often didn't give her the space and time to think and give an answer. I had a habit of asking a question and then, because she didn't have an immediate answer, I'd get frustrated and answer for her. Or, I'd ask another question, or try to dig a little deeper. This of course was infuriating to her because she felt she could never get an answer out. In my family, we were all very "quick to reply" and gave an answer or feedback as soon as we could. In fact, when my wife and I first got together, back when she was my girlfriend, she was awestruck at how...animated, my family meals were.

We'd argue, shout, talk over each other, swear, laugh and yell. 90% of the time it was in good faith, but we'd even have arguments at the family dinner table and things would get heated. That was just how I was used to talking with people. I didn't care if you disagreed with me or yelled at me, just let me get my point out.

Olivia is on the total opposite end of the spectrum. She

thought that the first meal she had with us was a genuine falling out. I had to explain it was just Sunday lunch. All that yelling and laughing and poking fun made me extremely resilient to people ignoring me and good at raising my voice. But I was lousy at listening.

I'm happy to say now that I think I've got a lot better at being quiet and listening. Now, when I ask Olivia a question, I will sit and wait patiently. For what seems like agonising minutes of silence, I'll just shut up and wait for her to respond. Since then, Olivia has said that it feels like I really am listening. The power of silence is in the space you're giving to the other person, and it is the best method I know for closing a deal.

When you give someone space and silence, they're searching for an answer. Some people might take a while to think of that answer, but they're working through it. I used to think that silence meant disapproval or contempt. But I've since learned that it gives the other party space to think. It's also the best method for getting the truth from someone else. Whether someone answers immediately or after a little while, silence is the best response you can give if their answer isn't good enough or what you wanted to hear.

For example, let's say you're closing a customer and you give them a pretty simple close. "We can get started today, we just need a signature and a deposit." You then shut up, stay quiet and let them breathe in the silence. While I've learned that silence isn't contempt or disapproval, it's still uncomfortable for other people. So they'll start searching for answers and giving them. Let's say that your customer responds with "well, it's a good offer. I'm just not sure..."

Most salespeople would jump back with "what aren't you sure about? What's the problem? Can we change it? Is there anything you do like?" They'll immediately go into objection mode and start turning the objection. Leaping to the "problem" like Steve Rogers on a grenade. But, that's exactly what you need to stop doing. When you were reading the previous paragraphs, you might have been thinking "Mike's dumb. I'd know when to shut up. If I was talking to my partner, I'd know exactly when to listen." But I have seen time and time again, sentences like "I'm just not sure" become like deal hand-grenades that salespeople jump on. When in reality, the customer is just thinking. They're thinking out loud. Nowhere in that sentence is a decision. Nowhere in that sentence is a "no".

Just. Shut. Up.

For 5 minutes. Please please please shut your mouth. Let them work through the answer in their own time. Delight in the silence. Revel in the peace and quiet. If you've got kids, this might be the only quiet time you've got all day. Don't ruin it with feelings of defence and insecurity. Remember –

assume the sale. They're going to buy. They're just taking a different path to get there. But they are going to buy. Know what you want. What do you want them to say or do? Wait in silence until they do exactly what you need them to do.

If they have a real question or a real objection, they'll ask it. They will state the thing blocking their path to buying. You are on the same side as them. You're on the same side of the table. How would you react if a colleague or team member said "I'm not sure"? You'd give them some time and space to work out the question or roadblock in their head and get it out in the open. The customer continues. "What about X (objection), can you do something about that?" Here they are stating the real reason that they're hesitating. All because you gave them some time and space. The objection will be clear and open IF you give them time to tell you.

Another massive advantage to being quiet is you allow the customer to buy. The amount of sales calls I've lost because I wouldn't let the customer buy is horrifying to me. I see all the time salespeople trying the close the customer, and then refusing to let the customer talk. They just talk and talk and talk. They silence the customer with a barrage of word-diarrhoea and the customer never has the chance to say yes. My step-dad used to use this trick **all the time** on **salespeople**. He would let them get to the close and he'd be ready to buy. But he knew that salespeople can't help themselves. He'd wait for the close and respond with "hmmm, let me think about it" and the salesperson would **IMMEDIATELY** launch into 100 reasons why he should take it now and he shouldn't think about it. Chris Smith was a lot of things, but "being rushed" was not one of them. He used to tell me that he'd count from 1 – 30 in his head and every time the salesperson talked, he'd reset the clock. If they let him get to 30 seconds of silence and thinking time, he'd buy. But what usually happened, is that the salesperson would talk and talk and talk and wear themselves out. Imagine that – 30 seconds of silence would have resulted in a sale. But they couldn't go more than 1.

Buying is a 100% emotional decision

"I'm a logical person, I buy based on facts and don't make decisions (especially buying decisions) made on emotion." How often have you heard this? How often have you said this? I've got news I'm afraid. There is no such thing as a logical decision. Especially, a logical buying decision. And I can prove it. True logic is almost a philosophical ideal. Robots and computers are logical. They perform the exact outcome they're told to, based on pre-written information. Human logic is often compared to as the opposite of emotion. If someone is acting based on emotion, we say they're irrational. But it's really more complicated than that. Because emotion is so deeply ingrained in both our culture and our literal brains, that thinking "logically" is almost impossible when it comes to decisions. When people talk about being rational and logical, what they really mean is that they've got a very good way of justifying their actions and decisions. They're still making decisions based on emotion, feelings and illogical and irrational beliefs. When we do make a decision, we'll come up with 100 reasons why it was a good and sensible decision. We work backwards to talk about things like price, milage, resolution, processor speed etc. We add features to our purchasing decision AFTER we've made the decision to buy, or even actually bought. This is critical to understand. The decision to buy comes first, based on emotional reasons, and THEN the customer works backwards to justify their reasons to buy – usually coming up with sensible logical facts that would seem sensible and logical to other people.

Let's take selling a car. People love to talk about the logical, emotionless and rational based decisions they make to buying a car. So why then, are there so many car designs? If we really were emotionally secure logical decision makers, then there would be an optimal car choice for most people? Sure there are factors like family size, number of journeys you make in a day or how far you travel. But overall, there really shouldn't be a huge difference in which car almost every car owner buys. Any time a customer walks onto a car lot, they're choosing between make, model, colour, milage, features, price and a hundred other things. And this is where the key component comes in – how much do you care about the car? This question of "how much do you care?" is what informs your decision.

How much value do you place on the purchase of a car? For me personally, I don't care about cars. Usually I'll buy second hand and drive it until I run it into the ground. I see them as a massive financial liability and a necessary evil. When I'm stuck in traffic, I don't see the difference in being stuck in traffic in a £5000 car or a £150,000 car. Besides, any time I need to travel far I'll usually rent a car. And look at what I'm doing? I'm justifying my decision to purchase a certain kind of car. I'm giving lots of reasons and excuses for my purchase which I believe are sensible, smart and rational. I believe that my decision making is logical – but it's all based in emotion. It's not at all logical, it's emotive.

When you're closing a customer, I've said previously that "futures sell, features close" and you will move into logic. But it isn't true logic, it's their logic. When I say features close, I don't mean that you now just list off all the literal features of the sale. I mean that you need to explain the facts and process of buying to the customer. You need to move into their mode of thinking and reminding them how to buy. Tell them what to sign, tell them what to click. Tell them how they can get started and what the process is to buy. Make it a logical step-by-step play on how to move them to the next stage.

The customer doesn't want to look stupid-give good reasons to others

What most people mean by logical decisions, is that they're able to

a) Justify the purchase to themselves

b) Justify the purchase to others

More than anything, people don't want to be disliked. That fear of being disliked is pretty much the driving force behind most decisions. And looking stupid or foolish is one of the ways we can experience being disliked. We don't want people to pity us, call us stupid or make fun of us for the decisions we make. So we'll make sure that every purchase we make, has a ton of "other people will understand why I bought this" statements included in it.

Surely not all humans are so shallow and insecure that all decisions revolve around wanting other people to like us?! Sounds pretty nihilistic. But remember, this is only the justification part. We do want to make decisions based on our own goals and needs and desires. But, we worry when buying "what will someone else say if they challenge my purchase?" What we want with every purchase, isn't just a good reason for us to buy it, we want a good reason for our friends and family (and even strangers) for us to buy it too.

When I was very ill during 2021, I spent time in hospital

and had several operations and ward stays back-to-back. I was diagnosed with cancer at the age of 33 and thought "I need to make sure I'm always as fit as I can be" so I bought a blender. And I bought what I thought was a pretty good one. In truth deep down, I'd always wanted one. I love smoothies and milkshakes and now this was the perfect opportunity to get one. Who spends almost £500 on a blender?! Well, Mike has cancer so... Ah right, in that case it's totally justifiable.

I wanted one, but I made sure I had a ton of "excuses" to buy one in the back of my mind. So that when people asked me "why did you buy this?" I at least had something half decent to give them in response. Is it sad and needy to feel the need to justify a purchase to other people? Do they even really care? It's my money isn't it? Absolutely. But as we've explored throughout this entire book, humans don't quite work that way. The story and reasons I tell myself are what really matter. I need the excuses and reasons and justifications. I don't want to look or feel stupid. Even if people don't ever ask or challenge my decisions, I want to have a load of reasons why I bought, lined up in the back of my mind. The truth is that I wanted the blender, and that's the hardest truth to accept. Just admit that you want it, and the reasons don't even have to make sense. BUT – we always want to have reasons that others might accept with every purchase.

When you're selling, you need to understand that the person buying isn't just buying for themselves. Even if deep down they're buying based on gut feeling, they'll want to have a handful of "external justifications" to present to others or even themselves, when it comes to evaluating their decision to buy. While personally I never go as far as to say things like "what will your friends think?" or "imagine how your family will feel when..." because I think they're cheap. But the customer is thinking "how would I justify this purchase to my family or friends? How would I convince them that I made a good decision?"

During the close, make sure that they have reasons that they can repeat, as to why they're buying. Sometimes during the sales process, that's as easy as asking "why are you talking to me? What made you make the call today? Why are we talking now?" and then listening to those reasons. Those are the reasons they want to buy. Then when we're closing, reframing their answers and repeating back their reasons "are you still looking to [answer]?" If they agree, then they're committed and now it's just a case of getting the deal.

Closing is so important that I'd hate you to miss out just because you forgot something simple. Head over to sellfuturesnotfeatures.com/workbook and get our Closing Cheatsheet sent straight to your inbox.

Closing needs

Sell Futures, Not Features

In order to close the deal, you need to have 5 things. Even if it's the greatest product in the world and the customer is super keen, without these 5 things you'll never ever be able to get the sale.

Buyer awareness

- ☐ Urgency
- ☐ Written offer
- ☐ Confidence in the product
- ☐ Confidence in you

I tend to treat these 5 things as checkmarks on a checklist. As I'm selling and closing, I'll make sure that I've either offered or asked the above checkpoints before I know that I can physically get the customer to buy.

1. Buyer awareness

This means that you need the to talking to the buyer AND they need to be able to make a decision. At the simplest level, you need to at least be talking to the decision maker. I have seen hundreds of businesses pitch to managers, employees, directors and other people, knowing full well that none of them can buy. How often have you heard "that all looks great, I just need to run it past my manager first"?

If you hear that ever, that's your fault. The reason we qualify leads is to make sure that we're talking to the decision maker. We talk to Batman, not Robin (shoutout to Troy from Agency Mavericks for teaching me that one). I'll talk about how to handle this later if you either didn't ask for the decision maker or they lied to you and told you that they were.

You need the buyer to be in front of you – categorically without question.

2. Urgency

People shy away from urgency because they're worried it causes pressure. People don't like the idea of being pressured into buying. The idea of the pressure-based salesman is an overly negative stereotype. As I've talked about earlier, you should be pressuring your customers. They should know that there is a negative consequence if they don't act now. The urgency for the close needs to be stated to the customer in order to drive them to take action.

3. Written offer

This doesn't mean a 40-page contract. It means that you need to have SOEMTHING in place that shows what both parties agree to do. Most of my contracts are a 1-page document with what we're delivering, when, how, what the investment is and what both parties agree to supply. It has a space for 2 signatures and a link to a deposit. Make sure you have a written document outlining the sale.

4. Confidence in the product

I've often said that if customers don't want to buy, they won't. There isn't a lot you can do about it. You could deliver a great pitch and perfect sales message, but if ultimately they don't feel that the product/service can help – you're stuck. You need to make sure that they are confident that the product can help them and that they're confident it will live up to their expectations. Don't overcomplicate this. "Are you confident that our accelerator programme could help you and your business?"

5. Confidence in you

Lastly, they must believe that YOU are doing the right thing. We've all shied away from products, not because we don't trust the product, but because we don't trust the seller. Ever seen a camera or games console for super cheap on an e-commerce website you've never heard of? You believe that the camera or product would be awesome, but you do not trust the person selling the product. In real life and face to face sales where you're dealing with people, they have to trust you. They must have confidence that you've got their best interests at heart. "Do you have confidence in me?" is a fantastic question to ask.

The reason these 5 things are so important, is because often these things are REALLY why the customer doesn't want to buy. But they'll come up with excuses often framed as objections. Without these 5 key parts of a close, you can't close. Get the buyer on the call, make sure there's urgency, have a written offer and make sure they're confident in you and the product.

Never ever ever return to selling

Just before we wrap up this chapter, I want to touch on what I think is THE biggest mistake I see when people try to close. It's not not having the buyer on the call, it's not failing to apply pressure or staying quiet. It's not memorising every close and objection turn. It's when I see sellers, return to selling.

Have you ever watched Dragons Den or Shark Tank and seen the entrepreneur (still winds me up when they're called that when they're pre-revenue) face a difficult question or concern from an investor, and the entrepreneur goes on a long diatribe about why that's wrong and how great the product is...That's called RTS. Return To Selling. And it'll kill every deal you work on UNLESS you stop doing it.

Selling and closing are very distinct parts of the process. Selling is transferring enthusiasm. Selling is working out if it makes sense for two parties to work together. Closing is the exchange. Closing IS the deal.

Imagine seeing a trailer for a movie and deciding that you really want to see it. That trailer IS the sales process. It is the transference of enthusiasm and to you, it makes sense to go see it. You send your friends a few texts and get the conversation going. You send them a YouTube link to the trailer and they agree it looks good. So you ask them to go to the movie with you. Then it hits you, from all angles. "What

312

time shall we see it? I can't do Wednesdays after 4pm or Thursdays before 4pm. How shall we all get there, should we share a ride? Can I bring a friend? What cinema shall we see it at? Do we want to eat before or after" Ugh! It'd be so much easier if people just did as you told them to!

All of those points raised are similar to the objections that customers and leads give. Would explaining the trailer to them or telling them how excited you are about it, make those questions any easier to answer? No of course not! So why do people insist on going back to selling, when they're IN the close?

If you've followed this book, you've asked them if they want help and told them what the close is. You're in the close when you decide you're in the close. If the customer, investor, lead etc. still has questions, you want to answer them in a polite, firm and enthusiastic manner. Here's another example. In Dragons Den, there was a product for saving money by reducing water usage in the home. Not a sexy product by any means, but a potential money maker and something that's relatively easy to sell.

The Dragons started asking questions as you do, about the company. Revenue, sales, the balance sheet etc. and then they got to the point where they were challenging the product and the percentage split that the entrepreneur wanted. For those that have never seen Dragons Den or Shark Tank, the basic idea is that I have a business and I go on TV to pitch to 5 investors and they like the idea enough to invest. The investor gives $X to the entrepreneur and gets X% of the business in return.

During this pitch for the home water saver product, the Dragons started to question how solid the product was i.e. how reliable it was AND the performance of the business. Here's a hint: whenever someone is questioning the product, it means they're INTERESTED. They wouldn't be asking questions if they weren't. They haven't made their mind up, they want to see if it's worth their time and money. And the entrepreneur presenting COULD NOT understand this. Every time a question came up, he'd refer to the product and start telling them about how brilliant it was. Rather than listening to the questions and agreeing with the investors, he made it harder and harder for them to get the answer they were looking for. This might seem difficult to understand WHY someone would do this. Especially in the cold light of written word "surely if someone asked a question about the product, they'd just answer it?" and the reality is that no, most salespeople will continue talking about the product rather than answering the question. It's like watching a car accident in slow motion.

Then, and this happens more frequently than I'd like, the investors made an offer! But the entrepreneur was so wrapped

314

up in the product and sales mode, that he refused to close. It was like your friends asking what time the film was, and you replying with another explanation of what the film was about.

It really can be that simple. When someone is challenging you, it means they're interested. "But Mike, doesn't a water saver mean that water companies will lose money?" That might sound inherently negative to one person, or positive to another. That IS an objection. So answer it – listen, agree, close. Don't go back to telling me how brilliant the product is.

When someone can't answer a question in an honest and straightforward manner, and talks around an answer, we have a word for that. Bullshit. And customers can smell it from a mile off. Be direct, respond honestly and agree with them. Take it in good humour, be humble and you'll be surprised at the response you get. I've even had people on a call tell me "you're just another one of those information marketers that sprouts bullshit and regurgitates other people's content aren't you?"

I had a choice to either be defensive, or agree with them. Here's the funny thing. When you agree with people, it lowers their defences AND yours. It removes credence and power. Even better, go one step further and make more fun of yourself. "Not only that, but I'm a lousy golfer too". It totally disarms people. Lots of people see objections as attacks and "answering objections" as a time to comeback and defend. It's not that at all. It's a chance to LISTEN. Listen to the customer, listen to their fears, listen to the product feedback. We have a saying at Sell Your Service which is:

"Anything anyone says, is a direct reflection of themselves."

When someone objects, or gives feedback or asks a question, it's a reflection of them and their world. They're not telling you something about you, they're telling you something about themselves. And if you listen and remove your ego and pause before you answer, you'll find that you can find things to agree on and close. Remember, in order to reach an agreement, both parties have to agree. Don't go back to selling when you're in the close.

Close and close again

Let's end this chapter, before heading into a bunch of my favourite close examples, with the ultimate piece of advice I have on closing. You can't make someone buy something that they don't want. But, if you are close to a sale, then remember to close and close again. Some people remember this as ABC. Always Be Closing. However I often see even the cockiest and self-assured salespeople fall at this hurdle. When the customer says no, and you respond, end each sentence with your close. End each sentence asking if they want to get started, or to sign here, or to take your items over to the cash register.

The last person who speaks to the customer, gets the sale.

If you don't close the customer there and then, the next person will. Don't take this as an endorsement of hard-sell tactics. Take it as a statement that if you don't get this sale, the next person will. The most you have to lose is a little pride. It'll feel awkward at first, but remember to assume the sale. Even if the customer is playing hard to get. End each sentence with the close – which is to say, end each sentence with the next step.

"I know, it's a lot of money. Sign here and we can get started."

"Well we're more than happy to change the delivery date. And the colour can be confirmed later down the line. Sign here and we can get started today."

"It looks to me like there are 10 reasons to buy and only 2 to stay where you are. Is it fair to say that you're still looking to get these taken care of? Then sign here and we can get started straight away."

I want to repeat the close so much, that my customers start to predict it. Trust me, they're not counting and it will sound more natural to them than it feels when you say it. This is also the secret key to ALL closing. Lots of people will teach you clever closes and conversations and questions to ask the customer, but they never ever remind you that it's not about answering the question or overcoming the objection. It's about telling them what the next step is. You could be the world's best "objection turner" and convince fish that they need scuba tanks. But if you can't get them to sign on the line, then it's all for nothing. Remind them over and over that in order to start benefiting from working with you, they need to sign and pay. Simple as that. And human beings are funny. We overthink and overcomplicate things, you have NO idea what the buyer is thinking. Their head could be swimming in thoughts and emotions, if you clearly identify what the next step is, after an objection, then they're more likely to buy.

Next up to finish this book, I want to cover off my top 6 closes for getting the customer to buy.

Summary:

- Money, cost and price aren't objections. They're problems to agree with, accept and move past. Don't get hung up on them

- An objection ISN'T an argument against you. It's the customer asking for help justifying this purchase even though they have reservations. It's a BUYING signal

- Closing is a game of logic and for straight shooters. Ask honest questions and get honest answers. Get to the root of the objection and work with them to overcome it

- Don't ever return to selling. Once you're in the close, continue to close. Listen to objections, turn them and close   again

Chapter 8 - My Top 12 Closes

- Benjamin Franklin (Jim from The Office, pros and cons)
- Why are you still talking to me?
- I agree, sign here.
- How motivated are you to…?
- We could look at the $15,000 version?
- I don't have any more money to give you.
- You don't need to worry about the price.
- Everything is expensive
- Do you trust me, and the product?
- We're still under budget
- What would be the worst thing that happened, if you made a decision
- If your partner is anything like mine…
- Had it not been for…
- What's your REAL concern here?
- Sooner or later you're going to need this
- I am simply in a hurry to help. My persistence is just because I want to help you get over the line
- I need some time to think about this

Benjamin Franklin (Jim from The Office - pros and cons)

This close is called the Ben Franklin close. Not because it involves you sleeping with multiple servants, but because it's based on a habit that Ben had of writing a pros and cons list. Jim from The US Office also has this habit.

The reason I love this close, is because it's usually my first port of call to respond to hesitations and objections (after the standard "I agree, sign here" close). As we've mentioned before; feelings sell, logic closes. This presents the offer and sale in a logical, thought-out fashion AND it gets the customer to sell to themselves. Let's say that your customer is clearly still on the fence.

Customer: I'm just not sure…

You: OK, I totally understand that. Can we do a quick pros and cons list? Ben Franklin was a hell of a lot smarter than me and he used this method all the time. I think it could help.

Customer: OK

You: I'm going to make two columns and label them PRO and CON. And let's both think of as many pros and cons for buying, as we can think of. To make it fair, I'll give as many cons as you do. This way, we'll be able to objectively see whether this is a good choice for you? How does that sound?

Customer: That sounds good!

Now, you just take turns listing pros and cons. The

customer lists a pro, you list a pro. The customer lists a con, you list a con. Start off by listing pros, or reasons FOR buying the product, then ask for a con. The funny thing, is that they WON'T be able to think of more than 3 to 4 cons, MAX. This is because there are only ever 4 cons to buying something:

- ⬚ Time investment
- ⬚ Financial investment
- ⬚ Fear of change
- ⬚ Risk/fear of failure

9/10 the customer will list money or price being their first and biggest con. I like to ALWAYS list the time investment as my first con saying "it's also probably going to take up some of your time to start with." And then we go back to listing pros. Another cool thing, is that the first pro they list is also the REASON that they want to buy. They're telling you exactly what their biggest takeaway is, this is golden to know. And eventually, they won't be able to list any more cons. If they do stop listing cons, just say to them "well, let's list another pro and maybe the cons will come up later." They never do. You will always have more pros than cons. But now the CUSTOMER is working through this decision too, they're arguing themselves into buying. When they can no longer list any pros, just turn to them and calmly say "well Mrs. Customer, it seems to me that there are 14 reasons why you SHOULD buy and only 2 why you shouldn't. And I think you can see the benefit in [top pro reason]. So should we get started? Sign here and what's the long number on your credit card?"

This method is easy, low stress but applies the right amount of pressure to the customer. It shows them that they're finding reasons to buy, rather than reasons to not buy.

Why are you still talking to me?

I want you to imagine that you're selling a TV. You're a sales assistant at a retailer like John Lewis or Target. The customer is talking to you and you're about to close a £1000 TV sale. But then they come up with the ultimate dick move.

"Amazon/Best Buy/Currys are selling this exact model for cheaper. Can you match it?"

Now usually, for a product like this which is a commodity, big box stores would do price matching or discounts. But I want to use a TV as an example to show that you don't HAVE to discount. If you're selling a service especially (and this still works with commodities), you never ever ever want to discount or even ACKNOWLEDGE the competition.

As soon as you justify their objection and bring price and competition into the conversation, you've lost them. Instead, I want to completely disarm them and get them to tell me why they'd buy from me. And what I do, is ask "So why are you looking to buy from us today?" They are here for a reason, they're here because on some level, they're looking to buy from you. If everything else is the same – product, features, model etc. Then apart from the price, they are here talking to you. So what is it that is compelling them to buy from you?

I once had a sales rep ask me this exact question, and it completely threw me off. I was looking to buy a new TV, and despite pretty good warranties in the UK and Europe, I wasn't going to get a replacement/refund for my previous TV which had broken. The store I had bought my first TV from, was doing anything and everything they could to weasel out of their contract. So I decided to go to John Lewis instead. I had previously bought from a store called Currys, but their service reps were not at all interested in helping me and frankly I couldn't be bothered dealing with it anymore. So I headed to John Lewis. For those who don't know, JL is almost always more expensive. They sell very nice stuff, but even their "like for like" tends to be more expensive. Now JL also has a policy called "never knowingly undersold" where they do price match for the exact same product. But they don't (as far as I'm aware) price match online e-tailers like Amazon. So, I was in a classic conundrum of who to buy from. Amazon was cheaper, but I was in the store right now with John Lewis. An argument could be made that at least in store I'd be able to walk away with the model today. But Amazon is fast approaching same day delivery for almost all its products. So when talking to the "partner" (as they call employees at John

Lewis), I said "Amazon does have this model cheaper" and without skipping a beat, almost like he was agreeing with me but ignoring me at the same time, the partner said "and so why are you talking to us today?"

He said it calmly, with a very friendly tone and a smile. He didn't repeat the question or talk around it AND he stayed quiet after he asked. Almost without thinking I responded with "because I don't trust Amazon delivering something like this. Plus I trust John Lewis and I know if something goes wrong you'll fix it..." I didn't know it, but I had just closed myself. He asked me to justify my decision to him. Most sales people would hear an objection like "XYZ has it cheaper or different down the road/online" and immediately go into defensive mode, talking about the features (which is totally counter-intuitive because if both sellers have the same model why would they talk about the product if it's the same – but it happens, just pay attention and you'll see it happens), or they'll talk about their policies and how the other seller is unreliable etc.

Don't worry about any of that. Ask them, "so why are you talking to me today?" They're here for a reason and that reason is why they're going to buy from you.

I agree, sign here

This is my most standard close. It's based on 3 principles.

- ▪ The customer isn't saying no

324

▢ In order to reach an agreement, both parties have to agree

▢ Tell them what the next steps are

All too often when we learn closes or how to close customers, we're given a list of closes similar to this one. And we read and think "holy cow, these are genius! But how am I going to remember all of these?" This close trumps all other closes with just how simple it is.

Point number 1. The customer isn't saying no. When someone gives you an objection, or complains about the price, you need to understand that they haven't said no. When the customer says "this is a crazy price! It's so much money!" or "I can't believe we're having to buy this" they're not saying no. They're giving an objection (kind of) or complaining, but they're not saying no.

So we reach point number 2. In order to reach an agreement, both parties have to agree. This sounds obvious, and yet, the first thing out of a salesperson's mouth after hearing an objection or complain is usually – "I disagree".

"No Mrs. Customer! It's not expensive! It's a steal! You should be happy with this price!" All you're doing, is arguing with the customer. You're disagreeing with their statement. I know you think you're giving a good answer and that you want them to see your point of view. But it doesn't matter. You're still disagreeing with them.

It is a lot of money. It is crazy that they're having to buy this product. Listen to them, show that you're on their side and that you agree with them. The worry of course is that if you agree with them, they'll back out of the sale. They won't. Worried that they'll then ask for a discount? They won't. They're venting.

Which leads to point 3. Tell them what the next steps are. "Sign here".

How motivated are you to…?

This close can also be used as a qualification question, and it's a great reminder question to get someone over the fence. Objections are when someone wants to buy, but needs help to justify the transition.

"How motivated are you to…[blank]?"

What we're asking is "how important is this to you and how much of a priority is it?"

Ideally, by this point you know exactly what the core problem is that you're solving and what the core problem is that they're trying to fix. As a general rule, people tend to try and avoid pain and solve problems before they move towards a goal. So at the close stage, when you're asking how motivated someone is, it's often more powerful to ask them how motivated they are to fix a problem before reaching a goal.

For example:

326

"How important to you is it that we finally get your weight under control?"

"On a scale of 1 to 5, where do you land in terms of getting this fixed today?"

"How motivated are you to stop working so many hours? And spend more time with your family?"

Goal orientated closes can work well of course, but the pain of NOT fixing something needs to be higher than the relief of reaching a goal. This close also works extremely well as an email campaign follow up.

Upsell close - we could look at the $15,000 version?

Customer: I just don't know if this $8000 product is right for us...

You: We could look at the $15,000 version?

You read that right, they're not sure about the 8K version, so we're going to offer them the 15K version. This is called an "upsell close" and it works surprisingly well. No matter what the customer tells you their reason is (money, time, features, trust etc.), offer to show them what the more expensive version would be.

Even if they balk at the price, or say "if we're not going to buy the $8000 version, why would I want to see the $15,000 version!?" just reply with "I just want to make sure you know all your options."

Talk through the higher ticket option and all the

BENEFITS included. Faster results, easier delivery, less work for them, more automation etc. What we're doing is anchoring the idea that the service they're buying, costs less. And if they want they can always go higher. Here's the funny thing though, often people will buy the more expensive option when it's presented to them. It's a bit like seeing a box of cereal for $4 but seeing 3 boxes for $8. The more expensive option is a better deal and often the customer sees that too.

"So that's the $15,000 version. I just need a signature and a deposit for it and we can get started today..."

I don't have any more money to give you.

If the customer is really hounding for a discount or asking for too many features, a great close can be "I don't have any more money to give you." What this does is reframe what YOU are giving THEM.

Customer: I think you can do better on the price. Can we get it down to $10,000 and include the extra options?

You: Mr. Customer, I don't have any more money to give you.

The key to this close is a big smile, calm funny tone and try to make it playful. Remember that you can't reach an agreement if one party disagrees. And, you're never going to convince someone that they don't deserve the things they're asking for. However, we can show them that we're willing to give them everything they want, if they are willing to give back. What you're giving them is worth money. You don't have an infinite budget yourself, even for services or digital products, you have a budget. What you're delivering, costs you money. With this close, you're explaining that you have given them all you've got.

"Mr. Customer, I don't have any more money to give you. We can get started today, just sign here and pay the deposit."

You don't need to worry about the price

This is one of my favourite methods of people asking about the price too early. If you mention the price or they ask about the price before you are to fully close them, use this as a reply. "Mr customer, you don't need to worry about the price, until we have confirmed this is the right product for you."

If you are closing the customer and you are in a position to tell them the price, and they balk, repeat the same close and go over the deliverables and their level of confidence in the product. "Okay Mrs customer, you don't need to worry about the price, until we have confirmed that this is the right product for you. How confident are you that this is the right service to help you lose £50 by December?"

What this does is put the pressure of the close back onto the customer and makes sure that they confirmed that they are confident that this is the right service for them. It doesn't have to be price either. It could be times, product feature, or any other deliverable. Until they have confirmed that they think that this is the right product for them allow them to not worry about the price.

Everything is expensive

I've mentioned this close a few times in the book already. It's essentially another agreement close. It's important to understand that a customer saying that your product and service is expensive, is not them saying no. Just like someone saying that a flight to New Zealand which takes 24 hours, is a long time, they are correct. But it is not them saying no.

Customer: wow! $13,982.15 is a lot of money! That's expensive!

You: I agree! Everything is expensive nowadays. I'm paying too much for my mortgage and my electricity bills. Why don't we sign here, and let's get started today.

You could even add something such as "before the price goes up again!" Out of all of the closes and objection turns, this is without a doubt my favourite.

Do you trust me, and the product?

In chapter 6 we talked about how the customer needs to trust you and the product. Without that, a deal can seem too good to be true. And I like to ask the customer if they are flip-flopping or dillydallying, "Mr customer, do you trust the product?" And then after they inevitably say yes, I asked them, "Do you trust me?" don't trust you or the product

Of course if the customer comes back saying something like "no I don't trust you" that's really important to get out into the air. And I would suggest calling it quits from there. Either from a perspective of them playing games with you, or they actually genuinely don't trust you or the product, it's very difficult to come back from this. I remember having a prospect tell me with a smile "no frankly Mike, I don't really trust you" and I decided to end the call. But just before I ended they said "well don't you want to convince me to trust you?" And this is a classic example of someone playing mind games. I pride myself on being a pretty straight shooter and I like honest dealings with honest people. I'm not interested in convincing you to trust me any more than convincing you to move house. Most people do trust you and trust the product, but we need to get them to answer this question honestly before we're willing to go on. When they inevitably answer yes, that's when you follow with "great let's sign here and get started today. What's your long credit card number?"

We're still under budget

if the customer gives you a budget, and your product is actually over budget, you can still close them by talking about how you are under budget. I know this sounds counterintuitive, but it's all about framing and perspective. Let's say that a customer has a £10,000 budget for a new car. When you give them the full price, and it comes to £13,589, you basically need to find £3589 worth of costs which are not to do with the car.

"Mr customer, we're still under budgetv, we've managed to find your car £9999. We've got the additional insurance and protection for £589. We've got your tax coming in at £1500 and the servicing and MOT for the next three years at £1500. In total that brings you to £13,589. Let's get started today. We just need a signature and a deposit."

If it transpires that they want absolutely everything for under £13,000, then gladly accept that they can look at another car or ask them which of the features they'd like to remove to get under their total budget. At first glance this might seem manipulative or changing the pricing to suit the offer, but in fact most people will gladly accept that their budget for a product might not be the entire budget for absolutely everything. And if it is then you can talk to them about reducing features or deliverability, negotiating with infantry or changing what they buy. But most people will gladly pay extra when they see that their main product is under budget and some of the bonus features (which they now won't want to give up) are "over" their budget.

What would be the worst thing that happens if you made a decision?

This is when I like to have a bit of fun with the customer. If they are going back and forth, and refusing to commit, I will ask them "what would be the worst thing that happens if you make a decision today?"

This is how we get there true objection out of them. It's the best way to uncover the real reason that they don't want to buy. Whatever the reason is that they give, they will almost immediately discredit themselves when they say out loud. More often than not they'll say something like "I'm worried that I won't get anything out of the programme, but now that I say out loud, that just sounds silly".

Whenever I have used this objection turn, people have often thanked me for helping them uncover a silly limiting belief. And usually worrying about something that could happen, when is talked about out loud, makes it much easier to deal with. "Mr customer, what do you think is the worst thing that will happen if you made a decision today?"

"I'm worried that I'll be disappointed and I have made another bad decision."

"I totally understand that. And I'm not here to ditch you

after you join us, we have a robust guarantee and returns policy. But I'm here to help you get over the line. You know this is the right decision, we can get started today and you'll feel the benefits immediately. We just require a signature and a deposit."

If your partner is anything like mine...

How often have you gone through a call and at the end they have said "great, I just need to run this past my husband/ wife/ manager/ director/ psychic?" It's easily the phrase I find most irritating. Because deep down this is a stalling tactic, not a real close. So I have a few ways to turn this, but first it's important that at the start of every sales call, one of the first questions that you ask is "does anyone else need to be on the call today?" If they do but they can't make it, read book and reschedule. If they say no and that they are the sole decision-maker, then carry on.

But if someone still says to me "I just need to run this past X", the first thing out of my mouth is "great! Are they there now? Would they like to jump on the call?" You'd be surprised at how often people are able to grab someone quickly and run them through the details. If they can't, you have a few options. First, I'm pretty open and tell people that I've invested a lot of time and effort into my sales process, and I'd hate to have to train them to sell it to their confidant. "Mr customer, I think it's great that you will run this past your partner. I've invested a lot of time and resources into our pitch, and I'd hate to have to put that pressure on you to sell it in the way that I sell it. It just wouldn't be fair on you." And then I let them talk for a bit. Before following up with "and if your husband, wife, partner, director, or manager is anything like mine I know that they'll support the decision that you're going to make. So we get started today we just require a signature and a deposit."

If they continue to insist on getting someone else to run through the program, do not leave the call without a booked date and time for a second call with their partner. "Okay I can tell this is clearly important to you to get your partners sign off. Let's booking a time where I can run through any concerns that you and your partner might have. How does next Tuesday at 3 PM sound?"

The golden rule is that you if you ever have to leave a call without a close, get a time and date for the next call.

Had it not been for...

This is kind of similar to the "we are still under budget" close from earlier. Often going through programs with customers will result in them wanting extra bells and whistles and features. But as Baron Mordo from Doctor Strange says "the bill comes due. Always."

Customers can often get swept up in adding features, extras and bonuses to their package. It's often a shock to them when their cost is over budget. Which is when we can remind them that their initial budget still holds true, just not for the additional features and requests which they have.

"Mr customer, we're still under budget. Had it not been for the alloys, tyre guards, sunroof and CD player, our offer would be well within your asking price. We can get this order started for you today, we just require a signature and a deposit."

Of course if they insist on having everything under budget, then simply ask them what they would like to remove in order to reduce the price. They'll never want to remove anything by the way.

What's your REAL concern here?

This is another way to get their true objection out. Often if they are stalling, you can tell that they either aren't challenging you (with an objection) or they aren't willing to make a decision there and then. Again candour can play a huge role in getting to the truth. "Mrs customer, what's your real concern here?"

Even with a seemingly obvious or factual objection such as timings or deliverability or with more surreal brought objections like trust and self-confidence. You want to get what their concern is out into the air. You can't turn something which you can't see.

Customer: need to think about this.

You: Mrs customer, what's your real concern here?

Customer: I've bought programs like this before, and I've walked away from them regretting buying them.

You: okay, that must be frustrating. So what's your concern?

Customer: I'm worried I don't have what it takes to make it worth my investment

you: I completely understand that. And I'm sorry I haven't covered this sooner. It's well worth thinking about, and you're right to question your level of work required. And what you need to know is that we are with you every step of the way. If you have a problem with the programme or the structure, we will work with you to overcome it.

This is also a great time to repeat the question "on a scale of 1 to 7, how confident are you that this program, product, service can help you?"

Sooner or later you're going to need this

"I agree, you could leave it till next quarter. But you and I both know that at some point you are going to need this program to increase your sales close rate. Sooner or later you're going to need to buy a sales programme. You could start in three months time, but the only difference is that you will be three months behind where you would have benefited starting today. We can get started today we just require a deposit and a signature."

Sell Futures, Not Features

This is another great close, for people who are stalling or saying they want to wait until next week, next month, et cetera. It's also why during your sales calls you need to get an indicator of how serious they are about pushing forward. During your sales calls when you qualify and sell to them, you want to ask something like "and how serious is this problem? Are you looking to get started sooner rather than later?" If they say that they aren't that interested or is not so severe that they wouldn't be willing to make a change today, it means the problem isn't severe enough, and therefore there isn't enough internal pressure.

I am simply in a hurry to help. My persistence is just because I want to help you get over the line

If you ever feel resistance and that the customer might think you are pressuring them, remind them that you are simply in a hurry to help them. "Mr customer please forgive my persistence, I'm just in a hurry to help." If you truly believe that your product is the best on the market and that you need to get into the hands of customers, then no one can argue against you being in a hurry to help.

If someone is resisting or hesitating but you know you can help them, remind them that you are on the same side as them, that you wouldn't be wasting your time or theirs, you're just in a hurry to help them and your job is to help them get over the line. You will be with them every step of the way, you won't abandon them and they will feel the benefits as soon as they buy. "I'm here to help, I'm just in a hurry to help you. I'm here to get you over the line, we can get started today. I just need a signature and a deposit."

I need some time to think about it

This is probably the most common objection I hear, that people just need to think about it. I've given you a few additional answers and closes to this objection. But my favourite close to this objection is "fantastic! While you've got me here on the call what questions did you have?" Typically people who say they need time to think about it are just stalling. As I mentioned if they absolutely cannot close on the call, then you need to book in another time and date. But more often than not when people have said to me I just need time to think about it and I have said to them while you've got me here what you want think about and that's when I will get true objections out of them and, we often managed to close people because I have allowed them to air their concerns to me.

Chapter 9 - Conclusion

At the start of this book I talked about a private workshop I was a part of, and how I felt an overwhelming sense of imposter syndrome. I wasn't good enough to be there, it was a fluke I even landed the opportunity, who am I to tell others how to sell things. That sense of despair about being discovered as a fraud is, in my opinion, the single biggest reason that salespeople and business owners don't dig deeper into what they're selling. They're more afraid of over-selling it, than they are of under-selling it. I believe that is tied to a deeper value that most humans have, where struggle and hardship are seen as virtues. It's as if we believe we're more moral as people, if we struggle to sell a product and it's more ethical to under-sell and make less money, by selling fewer products. So we downplay the benefits to working with us and buying from us, because deep down that might make us better people.

Hopefully this book and the Sell Futures, Not Features methodology has shown you, that not only are you more moral by selling to people. But that you can easily demonstrate how you can change someone's life, by talking about their life. Rather than focusing on yourself, the product or your business. If you focus on their life and their problems

340

and their goals, you're already a more interesting product. If you make someone's life better, you're solving a problem that's dear and close to them. I can't think of a more virtuous life than one dedicated to solving problems that other people can't or don't want to fix.

More than just sales

The sales process is more than just showing what a product is and asking if someone wants it. It's a journey of working alongside the customer and working with them, to solve a problem together. You're on their side. It's a collaborative process, not a battle or a negotiation. The product you sell has to be framed in the mind of the customer. It has to be part of a story that they tell themselves and see themselves living. Human beings are constantly thinking about themselves, rightly or wrongly. Our problems are very real to us and if you can be on their side, and believe in them and their dreams, and sympathise with their problems, you're immediately showing that you're not just in it for the money. If you start caring about them, you might find yourself actually caring about them.

It's also NOT about working with anyone who deems you a good fit for them. It's about making sure that they are the right customer for you. At my business, Sell Your Service, we turn down 99% of offers, customers, sales and leads. I don't think most people are right for me and my business. I don't want my team or my other customers working with 99% of the people I encounter. Sales is a collaboration. We're working out if WE are the right fit for EACH OTHER. I've had one too many selfish and brash customers who think that giving me money also entitles them to some kind of ownership over the way I work. I'd hate for you to fall victim to the same trap. Customers are not our bosses or owners. We are not their saviours or gurus. It's a collaborative process that sees us working together.

In closing, thank you for reading this book and taking the time to work on your sales process. You're doing the right thing, by trying to help more people. Getting more people to commit to their dreams and solve their problems, by involving you, is what makes the world a better place. Like most business owners (and humans in general), I still suffer from imposter syndrome. But the practices in this book have helped me balance them a little more, so that I think "maybe I can help people". I hope it can do the same for you.

I'd love to hear of any success stories from reading this book. If you have anything you'd like to share, please email me michael@sellyourservice.co.uk.

Remember, one final time, these kinds of books are more impactful when you write down your thoughts. Turn it from theory into practice. Download our entire 9 part roadmap to help you sell futures, not features for free at sellfuturesnotfeatures.com/workbook.

We'll send you the worksheets that accompany this book for free, straight to your email. Plus, you can follow the exercises along in this book and be one of the action takers.

Have courage, commit and take action.

Mike Killen